NIETZSCHE
A complete introduction

NIETZSCHE
A complete introduction

Roy Jackson

First published in Great Britain in 2014 by Hodder & Stoughton. An Hachette UK company.

First published in US in 2014 by The McGraw-Hill Companies, Inc.

Copyright © Roy Jackson 2014

The right of Roy Jackson to be identified as the Author of the Work has been asserted by her in accordance with the Copyright, Designs and Patents Act 1988.

Database right Hodder & Stoughton (makers)

The Teach Yourself name is a registered trademark of Hachette UK.

British Library Cataloguing in Publication Data: a catalogue record for this title is available from the British Library.

Paperback ISBN 978 1 444 79057 3

eBook ISBN 978 1 473 60151 2

Library of Congress Catalog Card Number: on file.

10 9 8 7 6 5 4 3 2 1

The publisher has used its best endeavours to ensure that any website addresses referred to in this book are correct and active at the time of going to press. However, the publisher and the author have no responsibility for the Websites and can make no guarantee that a site will remain live or that the content will remain relevant, decent or appropriate.

The publisher has made every effort to mark as such all words which it believes to be trademarks. The publisher should also like to make it clear that the presence of a word in the book, whether marked or unmarked, in no way affects its legal status as a trademark.

Every reasonable effort has been made by the publisher to trace the copyright holders of material in this book. Any errors or omissions should be notified in writing to the publisher, who will endeavour to rectify the situation for any reprints and future editions.

Cover image © Shutterstock

Typeset by Cenveo® Publisher Services.

Printed and bound in Great Britain by CPI Group (UK) Ltd, Croydon CR0 4YY.

Hodder & Stoughton policy is to use papers that are natural, renewable and recyclable products and made from wood grown in sustainable forests. The logging and manufacturing processes are expected to conform to the environmental regulations of the country of origin.

Hodder & Stoughton Ltd

338 Euston Road

London NW1 3BH

www.hodder.co.uk

Contents

Preface

Welcome to *Nietzsche – A complete introduction*.

My first encounter with Nietzsche was in his *Thus Spoke Zarathustra*. I was a first-year undergraduate at the time and, although there have been occasional frustrations and moments of despair, my love affair with Nietzsche's works has remained fairly consistent over the years.

I am currently Reader in Philosophy and Religion at the University of Gloucestershire in the UK. I have written books on Nietzsche, Plato, the philosophy of religion and Islamic philosophy. Previously, I taught philosophy and religion in schools and sixth forms, and was an A-level chief examiner. I have written A-level texts and accessible articles for *Dialogue* and *The Philosopher's Magazine*, and I give talks at schools and colleges.

Nothing gives me more satisfaction than teaching students about Nietzsche, especially when this results in a greater understanding and appreciation of what Nietzsche really says. This was also my main intention, and hope, in writing this book.

Roy Jackson

An eternal recurrence with Annette is reason enough for amor fati.

Introduction

Friedrich Nietzsche (1844–1900) is probably the most widely read philosopher in the modern world, yet he also continues to be the most misunderstood. His writings were almost totally ignored during his lifetime, and after his death his philosophy was neglected and badly translated until the mid-twentieth century. Until then his influence had been claimed in areas as diverse as vegetarianism, anarchism, Nazism and religious cultism. It is only more recently that Nietzsche has undergone something of a rehabilitation; and a deserved recognition has emerged that here was a man who ranks among the great and original thinkers of the modern age.

Nietzsche is most famous for his declaration that 'God is dead' and his consequent belief that we must therefore create a new man, a 'Superman'. With this declaration that 'God is dead', Nietzsche was the first philosopher fully to confront the prevailing loss of religious belief in Western Europe. What Nietzsche meant by this was that society no longer had a need for God, for He had outlived His usefulness. Nietzsche was therefore calling for humanity to stand on its own two feet without the support of faith or dogma of any kind. He was not only attacking religious faith but also a belief in objective values or truths. He was saying that we must choose our own values. The reason people persisted in a belief in God or truth, Nietzsche argued, was because of their reluctance to face the reality of their situation: it is a form of self-deception. Rather it is better to face and, indeed, to embrace, the temporary nature of existence and the apparent meaninglessness of life.

Nietzsche suffered from severe illnesses throughout much of his life, including migraines, which meant that he often lay in a darkened room, unable to leave his bed. He went insane in January 1889, and his illness and insanity may well have been the result of contracting syphilis, although he suffered from headaches even as a boy. Nietzsche, however, saw illness in a positive way, providing him with the inspiration to write and think: great works come from suffering, he believed. Indeed, he was able to write his greatest works during perhaps the times of his worse suffering, both physically and mentally. Works such as *Thus Spoke Zarathustra*, *Beyond Good and Evil* and *The Genealogy of Morals* were all written between 1883 and 1887.

A time of change

Nietzsche was born in what is now Germany (then Prussia) at a time of great change. The age of the telegraph had arrived in the year of Nietzsche's birth, Karl Marx's *Communist Manifesto* was published when Nietzsche was four and, in the same year, revolutions were breaking out across Europe with the growth in new values and ideas such as popular liberalism, nationalism and socialism. Over the next two decades Germany (under Bismarck) and Italy achieved political unification, Austria and Prussia eliminated feudalism and, in 1861, Russia freed the serfs. From the 1870s the second phase of the Industrial Revolution led to mass production of goods and the mechanization of society.

Importantly, from a religious perspective, belief in God was on the decline: Marx had declared it to be the opium of the masses and Charles Darwin's theory of evolution raised serious religious questions regarding the authority of the Bible. Nietzsche was to present a critical eye over these changes: he saw dangers in Enlightenment ideals, in increasing mechanization and secularization, in democracy and liberalism and in nihilism. In many respects, Nietzsche can be seen as a prophet of his time, yet also out of step with his time, as prophets often are. While many head like lemmings towards the cliff edge, singing the praises of science and political enlightenment, Nietzsche stands on the top of a high mountain and looks down from another perspective, one of caution and warning of the possible dangers of this new age.

Nietzsche is certainly the most controversial and notorious philosopher to have lived, as well as being one of the world's most interesting and scintillating thinkers you will come across, in the realms of philosophy at least. When people think of Nietzsche today they associate him with his harsh criticisms of religion, specifically Christianity, as well as his attack on the belief in 'another world'. Previous to his rehabilitation, however, many did not regard him as much of a philosopher at all but as someone who should be banned from the bookshelves. The reasons for this perception of Nietzsche will be unravelled as you read on, and even the current understanding of him can be considered as open to debate. The fact that today you can attend Nietzsche conferences, where he is discussed by serious and highly professional philosophers, should be sufficient evidence that here we are talking about Nietzsche as a very serious philosopher indeed.

On reading Nietzsche

The best way to get to know Nietzsche is to read him for yourself. His unusual style and lyrical approach to philosophy can, for the reader coming to him for the first time, be both unnerving and confusing, especially if that reader is used to the more conventional linear and discursive approach to argument. Even Nietzsche's mature and most coherent work can still leave the student searching for thematic hooks from which to hang the philosopher's cloak. One scholar of Nietzsche, Michael Tanner, remarked upon what is perhaps Nietzsche's best book, *Beyond Good and Evil*:

'If one goes through the text of Beyond Good and Evil *using a highlighter, one's likely to find that one has marked more than half the book. It comes as a shock when one rereads it a month later, say, and finds not only that one is reading many of the highlighted passages as if for the first time, but that one is scandalized by one's non-highlighting of other wonderful passages, and occasionally bewildered at what one did mark.'*

However, not only does Nietzsche present unambiguous themes in this text but also, with patience and perseverance, it can be seen that Nietzsche writes in a lucid and logical manner. When reading commentaries on Nietzsche, the reader must be aware that only relatively recently has he experienced a rehabilitation. You will not have to dip very far into the past to read works by scholars that rely upon poor translations of Nietzsche's work or take his published notes (not published by Nietzsche himself but by his anti-Semitic sister Elisabeth) as evidence of his final philosophy.

Nietzsche's works do not, on the whole, lend themselves to a straightforward understanding – using, as he does, metaphor, symbol, irony, sarcasm and 'in jokes'. This is certainly part of his attraction for readers, but also helps explain why his works were condemned by the academic community for their lack of academic rigour, detailed research, compartmentalization or high standards of source evidence.

If you take the time to read some of Nietzsche's works chronologically, you will see how he gradually develops his own voice, breaking away from the influence of the composer Richard Wagner and the philosopher Arthur Schopenhauer and developing a distinctive writing style that, though hard-hitting and poetic, was not regarded as the correct form to use for works of good philosophy. Nietzsche started writing in aphorisms: catchy passages varying in length from a single sentence to a short essay of several pages. This style may well be a result of Nietzsche's long walks in the mountains when he would stop at various points and jot down some idea or other. Whatever the reason, Nietzsche developed an undeserved reputation for writing in a jumbled and ill-considered fashion. In fact, Nietzsche always thought long and hard about the structure of his books, which, more recently, has caused analogies to be made between his writings and the sonata form in music. In fact, Nietzsche did also compose some music.

Yet aphorisms are a hazardous form of writing. A good aphorism strikes the reader as brilliant and memorable, whereas a bad aphorism will be quickly forgotten. Fortunately, Nietzsche was, on the whole, a brilliant aphorist. Yet the reader has to approach an aphorism differently from linear, discursive argument. Whereas the latter, if it is any good, flows along in a gradual manner, revealing its premises one by one, each aphorism, on the other hand, has to be treated as both self-contained and yet part of a greater whole. There are times when Nietzsche seems to slip in an aphorism that leaves the reader pondering over its relevance and it may be some time later in the book before that relevance becomes clear – if, that is, the reader can remember having read it! Aphorisms share a number of features with poetry, especially in their intention of engaging the reader on a personal level and requiring you to agree and be affected by what they are attempting to illuminate. Like good poetry, an aphorism can be enlightening and life changing. As Nietzsche comments in his work *Ecce Homo*, he writes so that his reader can dip into his books as if they were jumping into a glacial stream, that is, in and out quickly with the expectation that the experience will be remembered for some time to come.

However, because aphorisms are not simply intended to inform, describe and present a thesis, it is difficult for the student especially (as opposed to the casual reader) to know what is relevant, to know – referring to Michael Tanner's quote above – what to highlight. How can you argue with an aphorism? In *Thus Spoke Zarathustra*, Nietzsche says, 'He who writes in blood and aphorisms does not want to be read, he wants to be learned by heart.' (*TSZ*, Part 1, 'Of Reading and Writing'). Nietzsche – something of a child prodigy – would no doubt have had to commit many works, classics especially, to memory at his public school, Pforta. The advantage of this kind of study may not be immediately obvious, but those who still operate in this way argue that it pays in the future when the relevance can be seen. However, unless you intend Nietzsche to become your guide for life, the student can hardly be expected to learn Nietzsche's aphorisms by heart, nor would it particularly benefit your understanding in the more immediate term. A more pragmatic approach needs to be adopted.

In reading Nietzsche, it is difficult to find the 'real Nietzsche': that is, to find the answer to the question, what did Nietzsche really think? But if someone were to ask you what you really think, how sincerely could you answer that question? We all have a collection of thoughts and some are more certain than others, yet we also change our attitude and beliefs about things over time as we learn more. Nietzsche, like so many philosophers before and after him, is no exception to this. There seems to be a view by some that those 'in authority' cannot change their minds, but it could be said that the real thinker is someone who is open-minded enough to acknowledge that views can change. As you read Nietzsche, you will see that there are certain key topics that he keeps coming back to with new insights, amendments and better arguments. His views do change over time and, as such, his writings must be seen as a process, as thinking things through. This can prove to be very frustrating for the interpreter, but can also be something of an intellectual joy.

Another point to keep in mind when reading this book is that it is simply not possible to cover all aspects of Nietzsche's philosophy. His writings are wide-ranging indeed, covering such traditional topics as moral philosophy, politics, aesthetics (theory of art), epistemology (theory of knowledge) and religion. However, he also talks about history, women, food, sex, the self, mysticism, and so on, in an often bizarre and controversial manner that can leave the reader questioning the writer's grip on reality. On that point, although he did have a mental breakdown in 1889 from which he was never to recover, there is no reason to suppose that any of his writing previous to this is the product of an insane man: a genius and unconventional thinker, yes, but a madman, no. Having said that, as Nietzsche would readily admit, the line between madness and genius is very thin indeed.

On interpreting Nietzsche

If you get more involved in Nietzsche, perhaps studying him at university, doing some independent research or attending conferences, you will note that over the past 50 years or so two very distinct interpretive schools of philosophical interpretation of Nietzsche have developed, with differing approaches to studying his work. First, there is the **Continental approach**, which was dominant in French philosophy especially from the 1960s onwards and has been championed by such philosophical greats as Michel Foucault, Gilles Deleuze and Jacques Derrida (see Chapter 11). The Continental tradition, though something of a gross generalization to say this, concentrates more on Nietzsche's style: his playful and clever use of language, his poetic and imaginative use of metaphor and humour, and so on. This is not to say that content is not important, but that the content has to be understood within the context of Nietzsche's play on words and his use of the German language. The Continental tradition has generally defended Nietzsche as someone who is something of an existentialist, who argues for no objective moral values, and that knowledge is a matter of perspective.

Again, though something of a generalization, the Continental tradition sees Nietzsche as more radical and ahead of his time than the other philosophical school, the **analytic tradition**, would have him. Analytic philosophy is a multi-faceted phenomenon, but essentially what characterizes it from other traditions in philosophy is that it tends to align itself closely with the sciences and to focus on clarification of terms rather than produce whole systems of philosophy, which is more common in the European tradition.

In this sense, analytic philosophy may seem less ambitious but, at the same time, perhaps more realistic in achieving targets. Analytic philosophers – who are largely part of the Anglo-American world – see Nietzsche in a more traditional sense rather than as a radical existentialist figure.

In this work, it is hoped that both these traditions are given due worth, but ultimately such distinctions should not matter. The fact remains that Nietzsche has something to say, whether you are an adherent of a particular philosophical school or just someone who enjoys a good read.

How to use this book

This Complete Introduction from Teach Yourself ® includes a number of special boxed features, which have been developed to help you understand the subject more quickly and remember it more effectively. Throughout the book, you will find these indicated by the following icons.

The book includes concise **quotes** from other key sources. These will be useful for helping you understand different viewpoints on the subject, and they are fully referenced so that you can include them in essays if you are unable to get your hands on the source.

The **case study** is a more in-depth introduction to a particular example. There is at least one in most chapters, and they will provide good material for essays and class discussions.

The **key ideas** are highlighted throughout the book. If you only have half an hour to go before your exam, scanning through these would be a very good way of spending your time.

The **spotlight** boxes give you some light-hearted additional information that will liven up your learning.

The **fact-check** questions at the end of each chapter are designed to help you ensure that you have taken in the most important concepts from the chapter. If you find you are consistently getting several answers wrong, it may be worth trying to read more slowly, or taking notes as you go.

The **dig deeper** boxes give you ways to explore topics in greater depth than we are able to go to in this introductory-level book.

In addition, a list of **things to remember** will help you take away the key learning points from each chapter.

1

The young Nietzsche

In this chapter you will learn:

▶ *about Nietzsche's family and background*
▶ *about his education at school and university*
▶ *about his teaching career*
▶ *about his friendship with Jakob Burckhardt.*

Friedrich Nietzsche was born on 15 October 1844 in Röcken, a municipality in the district of Burgenlandkreis in Saxony-Anhalt in what is now Germany (at the time, it was part of powerful Prussia). Even today, Röcken is a small village with a population of fewer than 200. You can still see the house, the Pastor's House, where Nietzsche was born, and which has now become a museum. You can also visit the ancient church (one of the oldest in Saxony) where he was baptized, his village school, and the well-kept family grave where he is buried next to his sister Elisabeth and his parents. Röcken was surrounded by farms, and the nearest town, Lützen, was a half-hour walk away and was itself a very small market town.

The importance of a person's childhood on their views in maturity should never be underestimated. Nietzsche himself states clearly in his writings that our philosophies are moulded by our upbringing, which is why he is so critical of attempts by philosophers to be objective and to believe that they can ever step outside themselves. This chapter describes the background to Nietzsche's development as a philosopher: his childhood, education and early teaching career.

Nietzsche's background

'My time has not yet come, some are born posthumously. One day or other institutions will be needed in which people live and teach as I understand living and teaching: perhaps even chairs for the interpretation of Zarathustra will be established.'
Ecce Homo, 'Why I Write Such Excellent Books', Section 1, p. 69

Nietzsche's ancestry of some 200 German forebears has been traced back to the sixteenth century. None was an aristocrat and most were small tradesmen such as butchers and carpenters. However, he is also the heir of some 20 clergymen. Nietzsche's grandfather was a superintendent (the equivalent of a bishop) in the Lutheran Church, and the philosopher's father, Karl Ludwig, became pastor for the village. Friedrich's mother, Franziska Oehler, was the daughter of the Lutheran pastor of a neighbouring village.

The first five-and-a-half years of Nietzsche's life were spent in a parsonage, and even after that he was brought up in a pious environment.

It is curious to note that the philosopher who came to symbolize, more than any other, the rejection of religious dogma, was brought up within such an observant household. His philosophy has, as a result, been seen as a deliberate rebellion against a strict, oppressive and conformist upbringing. Yet the Lutheran Church resembles the Anglican Church more than a fundamentalist or puritan one. In fact, the Lutheran tradition has contributed greatly to German intellectual and cultural life and has encouraged cultural and social improvement. There is every indication that the young Friedrich had a happy and fulfilling childhood, and he never spoke in his writings of any kind of rebellion against his upbringing. If anything, the young Nietzsche was more strict and conformist than his peers.

'If I wage war on Christianity I have a right to do so, because I have never experienced anything disagreeable or frustrating from that direction – the most serious Christians have always been well-disposed towards me.'
Ecce Homo, 'Why I Am So Wise', Section 7, p. 48

Nietzsche's father, Karl Ludwig, was 30 years old when, in 1843, he married the 17-year-old Franziska Oehler. They named their first child Friedrich Wilhelm after the reigning King of Prussia, whose birthday he shared. After Friedrich, they had two more children: a daughter, Elisabeth, born in 1846, and a second son, Joseph, born in 1848. Nietzsche's two rather dotty aunts and Franziska's widowed mother also lived with the family.

By all accounts, Nietzsche's mother possessed a great deal of common sense and unquestioning piety, but had not been well educated. The first years of Nietzsche's life were quiet ones as the family settled down to their existence together. The descriptions of the house and its surroundings conjure up an idyllic setting, with a small farmyard, an orchard, a flower garden and ponds surrounded by willow trees. Here Nietzsche could fish and play, exercising his imagination as all children do. According to his sister Elisabeth's memoirs, Nietzsche took up talking rather late, to the extent that, at the age of two-and-a-half, his parents consulted a physician who suggested that the reason he hadn't spoken was because the family were so excessive in their devotion towards him that he did not feel the need to ask for anything. His first word, apparently, was 'Grandma', an indication of the female influence in the household, and by the age of four he began to read and write.

Tragedy strikes

Although Friedrich's childhood was, on the whole, a happy one, in 1849 tragedy struck with the death of his father. Karl Ludwig was only 36. A year later Nietzsche's younger brother also died. The traditional family existence was shattered, and they were compelled to leave Röcken to go to the nearby walled town of Naumburg. The young Friedrich now lived with his mother, sister, two maiden aunts and a maternal grandmother. Women, therefore, surrounded Nietzsche, and his younger sister, especially, doted upon him. Nietzsche's mother was still very young, but she was never to remarry.

Nietzsche had been very close to his father, and there has been much speculation over the psychological impact that his father's death, as well as the causes of his death, might have had upon the philosopher. There is little evidence to show why the pastor died so young, other than he was the victim of minor epileptic fits, and that he died from some kind of brain affliction. The speculation that he suffered from insanity is not substantiated, but it was a belief for Nietzsche that diseases are hereditary and that he was therefore destined for a short life himself. In his later writings, Nietzsche often paints an idealistic picture of his father. Perhaps the most famous account is in his work *Ecce Homo,* which Nietzsche wrote when he was 44 years of age:

'... he was delicate, lovable and morbid, like a being destined to pay this world only a passing visit – a gracious reminder of life rather than life itself.'

Ecce Homo, 'Why I Am So Wise', Section 1, p. 38

In many respects, life at Naumburg must have differed little from life at Röcken, for it too was a small town that saw or cared little for the outside world. Nietzsche was to live there until he was 14. His mother, as a result of legacies left by her own mother on her death in 1856, had the financial means to set up a home of her own.

Nietzsche attended the local boys' school, where he made his earliest friends, Wilhelm Pinder and Gustav Krug. Pinder, at the age of 14, wrote an autobiography in which he makes regular mention of Nietzsche, describing his initial encounter with the young Friedrich as one of the most important events in his life. The picture Wilhelm presents of the boy Nietzsche is of someone who loved solitude and had a pious, tender temperament while having a lively, inventive and independent mind. Significantly, his character is portrayed as someone who displayed the virtues of humility and gratitude and was preparing himself for a future vocation as a pastor. Pinder's father was a town councillor and lover of literature, and he would read Goethe to the three boys. Krug's father was an amateur musician, and we can detect Nietzsche's lifelong love of music originating here, as he took it upon himself to learn to play the piano.

Spotlight

As a child, Nietzsche, or 'Fritz' as he was known, was regarded as extremely pious and morally conscientious. He was once praised for giving his best toys to missionaries so that they could be given to children in Africa but, even then, Nietzsche was wracked with guilt in the knowledge that he had not actually given his best toys at all, and wished that he had given his 'box of cavalry'.

Nietzsche's education

In 1851 the three boyhood friends were transferred from the town school to the private preparatory school, where they remained until 1854. Here, Nietzsche received his first taste of Latin and Greek. Then they all went on to the higher school, the Domgymnasium. In 1858, when he was 14 years old, Nietzsche – no doubt due to his intellectual talents – was awarded a free boarding place at the exclusive and strict Pforta school. Nietzsche was studious, certainly, but he enjoyed outdoor activities such as walking, swimming and skating, and grew to be physically well built. However, he suffered from illnesses throughout most of his life and it was during these years that he began to suffer from headaches, which may have been linked to his short-sightedness and the many hours he spent reading and writing.

Pforta was disciplined and traditional. Pupils were awoken at 4 a.m., classes started at 6 a.m. and continued until 4 p.m. There were further classes in the evening. The school concentrated on classical subjects – especially Latin and Greek – rather than on mathematics and the sciences. As a pupil at Pforta, Nietzsche developed an enthusiasm for poetry, literature and music, and he formed a literary and musical society with some friends, called 'Germania'. The friends would meet regularly to read aloud the works they had written or composed. Nietzsche also enjoyed exploring scholarly criticism, which first led him to doubt the tenets of the Bible.

Spotlight

Though the Pforta curriculum focused on Latin and Greek, and Nietzsche went on to read philology, he never quite mastered any foreign language. His Latin translations were too obviously translated from the German and, although he spent a good deal of time in his later life in Italy, he could speak little Italian. Though considering himself a 'good European', he had little mastery of French, and virtually no English.

When he went to the University of Bonn in 1864 to read **philology** (the study of language and literature) and **theology**, he had already ceased to believe in the existence of God. At the university, Nietzsche soon abandoned the study of theology altogether, a subject which he had probably agreed to do only because of his mother's eagerness for him to become a pastor. Nietzsche never really settled in Bonn and in 1865 he decided to go to Leipzig University, where he became much more studious.

It was during the Leipzig years (1865–9) that Nietzsche experienced a series of life-changing encounters:

▶ It is likely that it was during this period that Nietzsche contracted syphilis after visiting a brothel. Syphilis was incurable and could result in a life of periodic illness, leading to insanity and early death.

▶ While wandering around a second-hand bookshop, Nietzsche came across *The World as Will and Idea* (1819) by the German philosopher Arthur Schopenhauer (1788–1860). Thus Nietzsche became a '**Schopenhauerian**': Schopenhauer's pessimistic view that the world is supported by an all-pervasive will that pays no attention to the concerns of humanity fitted well with Nietzsche's feelings at the time. He also read the *History of Materialism* (1867) by the philosopher and social scientist F.A. Lange (1828–75), which introduced Nietzsche to a form of Darwinism.

▶ On 28 October 1868, Nietzsche announced his 'conversion' to the hugely influential composer and musical theorist Richard Wagner (1813–83) after hearing a performance of the *Tristan* and *Meistersinger* preludes. Only 11 days later, he met Wagner in person. During that brief meeting, in which Wagner turned on the charm and entertained on the piano, Nietzsche discovered that Wagner was also a Schopenhauerian. Wagner was born the same year as Nietzsche's father and bore some resemblance to him, and so he became a father figure for Nietzsche.

Nietzsche's university professor considered him to be the finest student he had seen in 40 years. Consequently, Nietzsche was awarded his doctorate without examination and was recommended for a chair in classical philology at Basel University in 1869. At the age of 24, Nietzsche was already a university professor.

The professor

Between the ages of 6 and 34 – a total of 28 years – Nietzsche was never to leave the environs of the classroom for more than a few months during holiday periods. This was, therefore, a period of intense and cloistered learning and it is perhaps no wonder that Nietzsche was eventually to reject a career in academia. For the next ten years at Basel University, Nietzsche became less interested in philology and more enthusiastic about philosophy.

For Nietzsche, however, philosophy was not to be found by being immersed in books – which, essentially, was all that philology was concerned with – and he longed to expand his horizons. However, the lure of a salary and being able to support his mother was an important inducement in keeping the post.

Basel was a small, medieval town and, although it rested within Switzerland, was imbued with German culture. Basel was, however, in many ways quite different from the German cities Nietzsche was more used to, for this Swiss city-state was more cultured and less militaristic, with its university an important central focus.

> 'I am quite well aware of what kind of place this is ... a city which endeavours to promote the culture and education of its citizens in a manner so lavish as to be quite out of proportion to its size. It thus represents a comparison that is a shameful rebuke to much larger cities ... so much more is done for these things here than elsewhere.'
>
> Friedrich Nietzsche, quoted in Elisabeth Forster-Nietzsche, *The Young Nietzsche* (London: Heinemann, 1912), p. 208

The university asked him, on taking the post, to become a Swiss national so that he would not be called up for Prussian military service at any time, which would have interfered with his work. Nietzsche ceased to be a citizen of Prussia, but never succeeded in satisfying the residential requirements for Swiss citizenship. From 1869 onwards, Nietzsche remained stateless. Nonetheless, this did not prevent him from applying to be a nursing orderly for the Prussian forces during the **Franco-Prussian War**. It is quite possible that Nietzsche saw this as his opportunity to escape from the world of books, at least for a while. However, he caught diphtheria and ended up being nursed rather than being the nurse, after which he returned to teaching.

Despite his reservations, Nietzsche proved an able and popular teacher. Students spoke of his enthusiasm and their sense that this man had been transported through time from ancient Greece – such was his knowledge and explication of the subject. A famous incident in class was when he suggested that the students read the account of Achilles' shield in Homer's *Iliad* over the summer vacation. At the beginning of the next term, Nietzsche asked a student to describe Achilles' shield to him. The embarrassed student had not read the passage, however, and there followed ten minutes of silence during which Nietzsche paced up and down and appeared to be listening attentively. After the time had elapsed, Nietzsche thanked the student for the description and moved on!

Spotlight

During his time in Basel, Nietzsche cultivated his physical appearance. By most accounts, he was a smart dresser, almost something of a dandy. He began to cultivate his celebrated moustache that, in a famous photo of 1882, covered the whole of his mouth. There is another photo of Nietzsche with his mother, taken in 1890, which shows the moustache reaching down to his chin!

At Basel University, Nietzsche developed a strong affection for Jakob Burckhardt (1818–97), professor of the history of art and civilization. Burckhardt's had already published his greatest work, *The Civilization of the Renaissance in Italy* (1860), which continues to be important to this day. In it, Burckhardt outlined the historical transition from the Middle Ages to the **Renaissance** as a transformation from people's perception of themselves as belonging to a community to the idea of self-conscious individualism. When Nietzsche met him, Burckhardt had already been teaching at Basel for 26 years (and was to continue teaching there for another 24) and, although Nietzsche was in awe of this man, Burckhardt preferred a polite distance. Nietzsche's primary father figure, Wagner, however, now lived only 40 miles away in his villa called Tribschen on the shores of Lake Lucerne. In no time, Nietzsche became a regular weekend visitor there.

Case study: Jacob Burckhardt

Burckhardt's *The Civilization of the Renaissance in Italy* was widely significant and also very influential upon Nietzsche's own ideas. Never out of print since it was first published, it is a classic of the nineteenth century and gives the reader a vision of Italy, at times quite dark and haunting, as the birthplace of modern individualism, political calculation, science and scepticism.

In this work, Burckhardt identifies the Italian Renaissance of the fourteenth and fifteenth centuries as marking a profound break with the medieval past and the birth of modernity accompanying, as it does, a new sense of individualism. This new birth was, for Burckhardt, both good and bad: on the one hand, it resulted in the great creations of Raphael, Leonardo de Vinci and Michelangelo; on the other, it resulted in the violence, warfare, terror and bloodshed of the 30-year reign of the Borgias.

Burckhardt was quick to recognize Nietzsche's intellect and certainly valued him from an academic point of view, but this acknowledgement never stretched as far as friendship. This may have been due to some extent to the age difference – Burckhardt was of the same generation as Nietzsche's father – as well as differences in taste, for Burckhardt could never see what was so wonderful about Wagner. Burckhardt's coolness towards Nietzsche should not have been taken too personally, though, for it seemed that he was asocial towards most people. While an incredible intellect, multi-talented (he was also a poet, a playwright, an artist and a musician) and a charismatic teacher, he was something of a depressed and retiring character outside academia. Nonetheless, mutual admiration and respect were long lasting, and these two figures would often engage in intellectual conversations, which Nietzsche would recall with fondness.

From 1871 Nietzsche started to become seriously ill. This illness was to dog him for the rest of his life. He had suffered from headaches since childhood, but now they were mostly in the form of migraines so severe and relentless that he could not eat, and would have to remain in bed in a darkened room for days on end. These recurrent episodes always left him exhausted, and so it is all the more amazing that he was able to work so prolifically. During one absence from university due to his illness, he worked on his first book, *The Birth of Tragedy* (1871). Although loved by Wagnerians, as it sang the praises of the composer, it was attacked by academics as little more than Wagnerian propaganda and lacking in scholarly study.

Nietzsche's illnesses became steadily worse, forcing him to spend less time at the university. He was also becoming disillusioned with Wagner, whom he began to see as a sham philosopher. By now, Wagner had moved to Bayreuth, which put an end to the weekend visits. In 1878 Nietzsche wrote *Human, All Too Human*, a quite definitely anti-Wagnerian work, which caused Wagner to say that Nietzsche would one day thank him for not reading it. This work, though stylistically a great improvement on *The Birth of Tragedy*, was still viewed as lacking in intellectual rigour and coherence. This, together with increased bouts of severe illness and a loss of interest by students in his teaching, caused him to resign his university post on a small pension in 1879.

Key ideas

Lutheran: A follower of Lutheranism, which identifies itself with the theology of the German reforming theologian Martin Luther (1483–1546). It was Luther's efforts to reform the Roman Catholic Church that resulted in the Protestant Reformation.

Philology: The study of language and literature

Theology: The study of religious belief and practice

Schopenhauerian: A follower of the philosophy of Arthur Schopenhauer

Franco-Prussian War: A conflict between the Second French Empire and the kingdom of Prussia from 19 July 1870 until 10 May 1871

Renaissance: A cultural movement lasting roughly from the fourteenth until the seventeenth century, and which began in Italy

Things to remember

▶ Nietzsche was born on 15 October 1844, in Röcken, Germany.

▶ His father died when Nietzsche was only five years old. A year later his brother died.

▶ His childhood was, however, largely a happy one, and he was doted upon by his female relatives.

▶ As a child, Nietzsche was very religious, although after he became exposed to biblical criticism as a young teenager he began to question religious tenets.

▶ In his twenties, Nietzsche quite possibly contracted syphilis, which was to plague him for the rest of his life.

▶ Nietzsche published his first major work, *The Birth of Tragedy*, in 1871. It was not well received in the academic world.

▶ The year 1876 is significant for two reasons: it was when Nietzsche met Wagner for the final time, and it was also when Nietzsche published *Untimely Meditations*, in which he split from Schopenhauer's ideas.

Fact-check

1 In which year was Nietzsche born?
- **a** 1734
- **b** 1800
- **c** 1844
- **d** 1900

2 Nietzsche was bought up as which of the following?
- **a** Lutheran
- **b** Catholic
- **c** Atheist
- **d** Russian Orthodox

3 While wandering around a second-hand bookshop, which book did Nietzsche come across?
- **a** His own book *The Birth of Tragedy*
- **b** A book by Richard Wagner
- **c** The *Communist Manifesto* by Karl Marx
- **d** *The World as Will and Idea* by Arthur Schopenhauer

4 Which foreign languages were the main focus on the curriculum at Pforta school?
- **a** Greek and Latin
- **b** English and French
- **c** Persian and Arabic
- **d** Spanish and Italian

5 What is the study of philology?
- **a** Language and literature
- **b** Old bones
- **c** Greek culture
- **d** Greek religion

6 Which one of the following universities did Nietzsche *not* attend?
- **a** Bonn
- **b** Leipzig
- **c** Basel
- **d** Berlin

7 At what age did Nietzsche become a university professor?
  a 24
  b 34
  c 43
  d 19

8 In which war was Nietzsche a nursing orderly?
  a Austro-Hungarian War
  b First World War
  c Franco-Prussian War
  d Thirty Years' War

9 Who was Jacob Burckhardt?
  a A professor of the history of art and civilization at Basel University
  b A great composer
  c The husband of Nietzsche's sister
  d Nietzsche's doctor

10 What was the title of Nietzsche's first book?
  a *Human, All Too Human*
  b *The Birth of Tragedy*
  c *Thus Spoke Zarathustra*
  d *Ecce Homo*

Dig deeper

Jacob Burckhardt, *The Civilization of the Renaissance in Italy* (Oxford: SMK Books, 2012)

Elisabeth Forster-Nietzsche, *The Young Nietzsche* (London: Heinemann, 1912)

F.A. Lange, *History of Materialism: And Criticism of Its Present Importance, Vol. 1 of 3* (Hong Kong: Forgotten Books, 2012)

Carl Pletsch, *Young Nietzsche: Becoming a Genius* (NY: The Free Press, 1992)

2

Philosophical influences

Nietzsche's dissatisfaction with the academic world is reflected in his work. Although he did write some scholarly articles in the 1860s, he was a reluctant adherent to the accepted norms of the academic style. Nietzsche also considered himself to be something of a poet and a composer. He liked to improvise on the piano and wrote music himself. Certainly, he saw his writing as an outlet for his artistic capabilities and, indeed, much (though not all) of his philosophy is extremely poetic and dramatic. Nonetheless, in his early work especially, this can come across as evidence of an immaturity and a deflection from any kind of rigorous scholarly coherence that would have been expected of a university professor. Coupled with this, his relationship and blind love for Wagner infected his early writing.

This chapter discusses the major influence of Wagner on Nietzsche's development as a philosopher, as well as the influence of Schopenhauer, Plato and others.

The influence of Wagner

'All in all I could not have endured my youth without Wagnerian music. For I was condemned to Germans. If one wants to get free from an unendurable pressure one needs hashish. Very well, I needed Wagner. Wagner is the counter-poison to everything German par excellence – still poison, I do not dispute it.'

Ecce Homo, 'Why I Am So Clever', Section 6, p. 61

Wagner was always a controversial and larger-than-life figure. Although he had already written four operas, it was *Tannhauser* in 1845 that caused the most controversy. Because of its innovations in structure and technique, it both confused and shocked his audiences. He was also a political radical, taking an active part in the revolution in Germany in 1848, which required him to live in exile in Zurich, where he started composing the famous *Ring Cycle*. The political ban against Wagner was lifted in 1861 and he returned to Prussia. Despite marrying an actress in 1836, Wagner had a number of affairs, most notably with the daughter of the composer Liszt, Cosima von Bulow, whom he married in 1870.

Wagner was more than a composer, however. He was also a musical theorist, and his thought on political issues such as nationalism and social idealism greatly influenced the nineteenth century. His music was strongly nationalist, and he had also expressed clear anti-Semitism in his writings, making him an attractive composer for the Nazis. Despite this reputation, Wagner did effect a revolution in the theory and practice of operatic composition, and it was this factor that would have appealed to Nietzsche and his early belief that music acted as a salvation.

In retrospect, it seems surprising that someone as perceptive as Nietzsche seemed to be so taken in by the flamboyant ego of Wagner. It is said that, during Nietzsche's weekend visits to Tribschen, Wagner would behave as if in one of his own operas. Dressed extravagantly, with only his own music playing, he would waft across the gardens and corridors of his luxurious villa among busts of himself, talking mostly about himself! However, this picture is most likely an exaggeration, and Nietzsche did learn much from being in the company of Wagner, for he recognized the composer's ego as a need to dominate others, to exert his power over them. Undoubtedly, Wagner was a charismatic figure, and it is quite impressive what he could persuade others to do for him.

From studying Wagner, Nietzsche developed his own views on psychology and on humans' desire to dominate others. In this respect, Wagner's eccentricities were a minor irritation. However, during the early Leipzig years, Nietzsche's infatuation with Wagner and his willingness to sacrifice his own career, if need be, to serve under the composer came across only too obviously in his early writings, especially with his first major work, *The Birth of Tragedy*.

It was in Wagner's writings, especially in five essays published during 1849–51, that laid the basis for Nietzsche's early philosophy. Wagner wrote a series of works discussing his views on the relationship between art and life. Some of the most significant, in terms of influencing Nietzsche, were:

▶ **'Art and Revolution'** (July 1849)
Tracing the history of the arts, Wagner holds that the individual arts (music, drama, theatre, etc.) were once a complete and perfect whole. This art form existed only in the tragic drama of ancient Athens and disappeared when it split into its various components. After that time, and up until the present day, people looked to philosophy rather than art for an understanding of their world. Art in its highest and most perfect form is, therefore, pre-Christian.

▶ **'The Artwork of the Future'** (September 1849)
Here, Wagner argues that all the greatest inventions of humankind, from language to society, are a product of the *Volk* ('folk'). The *Volk* is more than a collection of individuals; it is the submersion of individual identity and ego and the resulting expression of a mystical group consciousness. The highest expression of this *Volk* consciousness is art, and Wagner makes a link between *Volk* art and nature. Therefore, the future of artwork is for all artists of all types to put aside their own individuality and ego (rather ironic coming from Wagner!) and the result will be a true expression of nature as art.

▶ **'Opera and Drama'** (January 1851)
This is not so much an essay as a full-scale book. The composer sings the praises of his forthcoming opera cycle *The Ring of the Nibelung* as an example of complete art, and criticizes the opera of his contemporaries such as Rossini.

▶ **'A Communication to My Friends'** (August 1851)
Wagner considers the faults and successes of his own previous works and explains why he feels the need for a new kind of musical drama. Wagner presents his own plan to produce a four-part musical drama – the *Ring Cycle* – as a model of perfect art. He advertises his intentions to present this work at some future festival.

THE BAYREUTH FESTIVAL OF 1876
This future festival became the Bayreuth Festival of 1876, which consisted of the complete first performance of Wagner's

Ring Cycle. It is a significant event in that it marks Nietzsche's realization that Wagner was not the great saviour he had envisioned. Attending the festival, Nietzsche was later to remark that he found the whole performance indicative of Wagner's German nationalism and anti-Semitism: two things Nietzsche found particularly distasteful. However, in 1871, when *The Birth of Tragedy* was published, Nietzsche was still very firmly in the grip of Wagner's charisma.

Case study: Wagner's music

It is something of a myth that Wagner was a late developer when it came to composing (a myth that Wagner himself encouraged). In fact, he had already decided in his teens that he wanted to be a composer of operas and, indeed, started work on his first composition. At this time, in the 1820s, there were three forms of contemporary opera:

▶ German romantic opera, and especially the works of Carl Weber (1786–1826) such as *Euryanthe* and *Oberon*, with an emphasis on supernatural events and a focus on the orchestra rather than the singing

▶ Italian opera, represented by the likes of Vincenzo Bellini (1801–35) and Gioachino Rossini (1792–1868), who tended to write more traditionally romantic love stories and concentrated more on the singing

▶ French opera, with composers such as Daniel Auber (1782–1871), who tended to write very long works with grand panoramic sets and a large cast, staging historical events – for example, the hugely successful five-act opera *Gustave III*, which concerns the assassination of the King of Sweden.

Wagner, for his part, decided to write three operas, each in these respective styles. His first full-length opera was *The Fairies* (1834), in the German romantic style; his second was *The Ban on Love* (1836), in the Italian style; and the third was *Rienzi* (1840), in the French style.

Wagner then decided that the French and Italian styles were 'decadent' (i.e. had reached their end), whereas there was more work to be done with the German romantic style. His next three operas, *The Flying Dutchman* (1841), *Tannhauser* (1845) and *Lohengrin* (1848), all encompassed and, indeed, developed beyond what had been achieved in this style.

But it is Wagner's later works, what are known as his 'mature operas', that make him stand out as the creator of a new form of opera, with his *Ring Cycle*, *Tristan and Isolde*, *The Mastersingers* and his final opera, *Parsifal*. These were *Gesamtkunstwerke*, 'total works of art' that aimed to combine drama, music, poetry and visual art.

Nietzsche intended his book *The Birth of Tragedy* (see Chapter 4) to be a manifesto for change, as a call for a revolution. He believed that humankind had lost all sense of purpose and was clinging on to religious and philosophical views that were no longer credible. He called for a return to the principles of Greek tragedy and devoted the final third of the book to the praise of Wagner as the new tragedian.

In this respect, the book failed completely. It was attacked severely by academics, although, not surprisingly, praised by Wagnerians. Nietzsche himself, in a preface to the book added in 1886, described it as badly written and confused. However, perhaps Nietzsche is too severe a critic of his own work. It has elements of originality and, most importantly, it raises the question of the importance of art in our understanding of the world and our place within it. Art, together with our instinctual side, can also provide us with insights that are not accessible through reason.

The more cynical critics of Nietzsche saw *The Birth of Tragedy* as little more than a publicity stunt for Wagner. Their criticisms are understandable, in that there did seem to be some mutual back-patting going on. Wagner, for his part, introduced Nietzsche to his publisher, while Nietzsche devoted a good deal of his book and his own time towards promoting Wagner as the new revolutionary, and, in so doing, laid the groundwork for the success of the Bayreuth Festival.

When, in 1872, Wagner left Tribschen and moved to Bayreuth, the relationship between the two mellowed. Nietzsche, despite growing doubts, remained a Wagnerian. In fact, Nietzsche's publicizing for the composer did not stop there, as is evident from the fourth of his *Untimely Meditations* written in 1876.

After a series of financial difficulties that were resolved only by the offer of a subsidy by King Ludwig, the festival was finally set for August 1876. The small town of Bayreuth was chosen, and Wagner engaged in an immense process of creative and exhausting industry to prepare for what was to be an incredible musical endeavour.

Spotlight

In the summer of 1874 Nietzsche decided to visit Wagner's house. This was the worst time Nietzsche could have chosen, for Wagner was not ready for interruptions as he had yet to complete his composition for the festival. Nietzsche annoyed Wagner intensely during this period, as may well have been his intention: he employed seemingly deliberate tactics to antagonize the composer, such as carrying a score of Brahms with him (Wagner hated Brahms) and even playing it on Wagner's own piano.

The festival was due to begin on 13 August with the first complete performance of the *The Ring of Nibelung*. *The Ring* consists of a lengthy prelude, followed by three musical tragedies: a 14-hour saga in total. The inspiration for this new myth derives from a number of old sagas, medieval German retellings and contemporary commentaries. Wagner's stated aim was to present his 'musical drama' (he was clear that this was not an opera, which he considered to be an example of how decadent art had become) to the *Volk*, an audience that would participate in the emotional purpose of the drama. He presented a vision of the Greek masses streaming in their thousands into the Athenian amphitheatre, and he imagined the same for Bayreuth. As it turned out, however, the first performance consisted of just the kind of people who would attend an opera: emperors, kings, barons and the upper-middle classes. Not surprisingly, this audience were hardly prepared to let their hair down to engage in ecstatic, mystical union.

Nietzsche, for his part, could have been at the centre of the whole enterprise if he had so wished, but he preferred to remain on the sidelines. He did sit through the first complete *Cycle,* but gave his tickets away for the rest of the festival – the second *Cycle* in late August and the third in early September. Nietzsche was later to write that his morose behaviour during the festival was because of his awareness that Wagner was not to be the saviour, after all. However, although disillusionment with Wagner was most likely a factor, Nietzsche's increasing ill health at that time would not have suited the activities of a music festival.

The influence of Schopenhauer

'I came across this book in old Rohn's second-hand bookshop, and taking it up very gingerly I turned over its pages. I know not what demon whispered to me: "Take this book home with you." At all events, contrary to my habit of not being too hasty in the purchase of books, I took it home. Back in my room I threw myself into the corner of the sofa with my booty, and began to allow that energetic and gloomy genius to work upon my mind.'

Friedrich Nietzsche, *Historisch-kritische Gesamtausgabe*
(Munich: Beck, 1933), III, pp. 297–8

Nietzsche's final meeting with Wagner was in Sorrento, Italy, in 1876. Their meeting was brief and polite but it was obvious to both of them that the friendship was over. That year, with the completion of his *Untimely Meditations*, also marked Nietzsche's split from the influence of the German philosopher Arthur Schopenhauer (1788–1860).

To understand Schopenhauer's and, indeed, Nietzsche's philosophy, it helps to have a brief account of the main philosophical themes that acted as a backdrop to German philosophy of the time. In all his writings, Nietzsche's assumes that his reader is already familiar with philosophy. This can often make reading Nietzsche very difficult if you wish to appreciate him at a deeper level. Only a brief outline of the major philosophers and their views can be presented here, but no thinker comes up with ideas in a vacuum. The importance of past thinkers on Nietzsche's philosophy must always be borne in mind. Nietzsche, in his writings, makes constant references to people like Kant, Schopenhauer, Plato and so on. Often, he is critical of them, but he is also indebted to them.

The influence of Plato

Much of ancient Greek philosophy, most notably the works of Plato (c.428–348 BCE), questioned the nature of existence: is what we can see with our senses (sight, touch, taste, hearing, feeling) actually what is? For example, you see trees and birds outside your window, but can you be sure that they really exist and that they are what we see them to be? Plato held that the world that we perceive with our senses is only appearance. Things are not as they appear to be and we are often deceived into thinking that we distinguish something when, in fact, we do not. In other words, our senses are unreliable. However, humankind has the gift of reason and it is with our rational capacity, our intellect, that we can determine what really exists.

This view that there are two worlds, the world or appearance and the world of reality, has also existed in many of the great religions and, inevitably, it has led to speculation over what the 'real' world consists of and how, if at all, it is possible to enter this real world. It is a view that is known in philosophy as dualism. For Plato, we gain access to the real world through the exercise of reason; for many religions, it is through faith or ritual practice. Plato was, therefore, a supporter of rationalism: he believed that the power of reason provides us with important knowledge about the world.

Descartes and Spinoza

The French philosopher René Descartes (1596–1650) expressed this dualism in a simpler manner; there are only two existent things: thinking substance (soul) and extended substance (matter). Descartes, however, was not overly concerned with which is 'more real' than the other, and nor did he satisfactorily address the important issue of how two very different kinds of substance can possibly interact with each other. The Dutch philosopher Baruch Spinoza (1632–77) responded to Descartes' dualism with his pantheism. For Spinoza, soul and matter are not 'substances', for there is only one substance in the whole universe, and that is God. Soul and matter, therefore, are merely expressions of God.

Locke and Berkeley

The debate between Descartes and Spinoza took on another form with the British philosophers John Locke (1632–1704) and Bishop George Berkeley (1685–1753). Locke is regarded as the founder of the philosophical school known as empiricism: our knowledge comes from our experience of the world; the mind at birth is a complete blank. In direct opposition to rationalism, Locke argued that all of our knowledge of the world comes through experience of the material world. There are just two sources of knowledge, ideas of sensation and ideas of reflection:

▶ **Ideas of sensation** are, at the basic level, when the mind, through the senses, perceives an object – its colour, shape, size and so on.

▶ **Ideas of reflection** are when the mind reflects upon the object that is perceived. This goes beyond mere perception, in which the subject forms associations with other objects that are either present or from memory, and is able to exercise his or her imagination.

The point Locke is making here is that the 'ideas' of mind, whether ideas of sensation or ideas of reflection, have their basis in the material world; they are not innate. Berkeley wrote in opposition to sceptics such as Locke by raising the question that, if, as Locke argues, our knowledge of the material world rests upon the ideas that we have in our heads, then why should we suppose that there is anything but the ideas in our heads? The material world would be unnecessary. If it did not exist, then it would not change our ideas one bit. Berkeley, therefore, concludes that there is no such thing as matter, only mind. This conclusion makes Berkeley the founder of the philosophical school of modern idealism: the position that gives a key role to the mind in the constitution of the world as it is experienced.

The question arises, however, as to where the ideas in the mind come from, if not from matter. Berkeley states that the ideas from the mind come directly from God. For Berkeley, too, there are two kinds of ideas:

▶ Those that we have no control over – for example, sights and sounds that are forced upon our consciousness; as these are not a product of our will, then they must be a product of some other will, which is God

▶ Those that we do have control over – for example, reflecting upon our ideas or exercising our imaginations.

Hume and Kant

The Scottish philosopher and empiricist David Hume (1711–76) asserted that our mind consists of impressions and ideas:

▶ **Impressions** are what Locke called 'ideas of sensation': objects, colours, sounds and so on, of the material world.

▶ **Ideas** are images of impressions that are formed from thinking and reasoning.

We can, therefore, have no ideas of anything unless we first receive an impression. For example, you may have an impression of fire and an impression of heat, so you then form the idea in your mind that fire *causes* heat. However, Hume argues, the *causation* does not exist in reality, only in our minds. Causation is based upon past experience, but that does not mean that fire will cause heat in the future. At best, we can only *suppose* that it will.

When the German philosopher Immanuel Kant (1724–1804) read Hume, it changed his life and he set about developing the foundation of modern German philosophy that had a direct influence upon Schopenhauer and Nietzsche. Kant agreed with

Hume that there are no innate ideas, but he did not accept that all knowledge is derived from experience. Whereas empiricism argues that our knowledge must conform to experience, Kant turned this around and argued that our experience must conform to our knowledge.

For example, an empiricist would argue that if you experience a stone falling to the floor many thousands of times then you suppose, based upon that experience, that it will fall to the floor the next time. It *may not*, of course, but it is the only knowledge we have to go on: our minds create the 'idea' that the stone will fall. Now, Kant is notoriously difficult and technical at the best of times but, put simply, he asks why we impose causation upon the stone. That is, why do we suppose that letting go of the stone will cause it to fall to the ground? Causation is not derived from the senses, and here Kant agrees with Hume, but then where *does* it come from? Kant argues that we humans impose an order upon the world; we impose causation, quantity, quality and so on, so that we may understand it. There are, therefore, two worlds:

▶ the world of **phenomena** or 'appearance'

▶ the world of **noumena** or 'reality'.

It is rather like wearing irremovable spectacles that make you see the world in a certain way. However, this is not how the world really is. The world of the noumenal we cannot see because we are limited in our perceptions. The inevitable conclusion Kant reached is that there is the world of appearance that we impose through our 'irremovable spectacles' and there is the world as it really is, which we cannot perceive.

Schopenhauer accepts Kant's view that there is a phenomenal world and a noumenal world. However, he believed that it is possible to know the noumenal:

▶ He equates the world of phenomena with Berkeley's ideas in the mind. Therefore, the world as it is perceived is the creation of the mind that perceives it. In other words, 'the world is my idea'.

- As Kant argues that if there is an 'apparent' world there must also be a real world, Schopenhauer equates the real world with the 'I' who has the idea.

Our knowledge of ourselves is obviously different from the knowledge we have of anyone or anything else. We know ourselves objectively in the same way that we know other phenomena in the world; that is, as a physical object, a body. We also have subjective knowledge, our inner consciousness, our feelings and desires. It is our inner selves that Schopenhauer calls 'will'. Therefore, the body is part of the phenomenal world, the world of appearance, and the will is in the noumenal form, the world of reality. We can sum this up thus:

- Ideas = appearance = body and other objects

- The 'I' that has the idea = reality = will.

The world is a duality. All things have both Will and Idea, even a stone. However, in the case of the stone, its Will has not attained a state of consciousness. Schopenhauer's concept of 'Will' should not be understood in the common sense as simply wanting something for oneself, for it is much more than that. It is the essence of what it means to be human.

Previous to Schopenhauer, much of the philosophical tradition places humankind as the thinking animal, as a rational, conscious being, but Schopenhauer saw consciousness as the mere surface of our minds. Under the conscious intellect is the unconscious Will, which is a striving, persistent force. On appearance it may seem that the intellect drives the Will, but it is, in fact, the other way round. When you desire something it is not because you have found a good reason to desire it, but, rather, that you desire something first and then establish reasons to cloak those desires. Therefore, it is pointless to appeal to people through logic. Rather, you must look to their desires, their self-interests.

Case study: Schopenhauer's pessimism

In Schopenhauer's view, every person embodies Will and the nature of Will is to survive. In the Darwinian sense of survival of the species, every individual is striving against the Will of others in a self-interested way. This inevitably results in conflict and suffering. Schopenhauer therefore sees the Will as essentially evil, and the only way out of this suffering and evil is the denial of the Will, a refusal to take part in the egotistical contest for domination of others. This can be achieved through the power of the conscious intellect, which is able to comprehend the nature of the Will and its effects. The result, by denying the Will (which is the only reality) and being left with ideas (which are not real), is extinction of the self. This philosophy now enters the realms of ascetic sainthood, and Schopenhauer reveals the influence of Buddhism upon him.

'...[O]nly the will is thing in itself... It is that of which all representation, all object, is the phenomenon, the visibility, the objectivity. It is the innermost essence, the kernel, of every particular thing and also of the whole.'
Arthur Schopenhauer, *The World as Will and Representation* vol. 1 (New York: Dover Publications, 1966), p. 110

Nietzsche, like Wagner, initially accepted the view that we should deny the Will, although he was later to doubt the practicality of such an activity. In fact, Schopenhauer himself was hardly the best model of the ascetic, for he loved the material pleasures that life had to offer.

Ultimately, the most important influence of Schopenhauer on Nietzsche amounts to three things:

1 Like Schopenhauer, Nietzsche presented the picture of the philosopher who will stop at nothing in the search for truth, however painful that might be.

2 Schopenhauer's style of writing, perhaps more than the content, had an influence on Nietzsche's own style and provided a demonstration that one can write philosophy and also write well.

3 Nietzsche seemingly (see Chapter 6 for the debate on this) adopted the primacy of the Will as the motivating force, and this became his famous doctrine of the will to power.

However, Nietzsche's will to power is in many respects different from Schopenhauer's Will, and Nietzsche was much more materialistic (that is, 'down-to-earth') in his philosophy than Schopenhauer's almost mystical views. Both Wagner and Schopenhauer, therefore, played an important part in Nietzsche's early works, but this influence dwindles as Nietzsche develops his own voice.

Key ideas

Dualism: the philosophical position that there are two worlds: the physical and the non-physical

Rationalism: the philosophical position that reason, the intellect, forms the basis for much of our knowledge

Empiricism: the philosophical position that we can acquire knowledge of the world through direct experience of the senses

Idealism: the importance of the mind in understanding what we can know about the world: at the most extreme, it argues that there is only the mind, no external world

Noumena: metaphysical beliefs about the soul, the cosmos and God, which are matters of faith rather than scientific, empirical knowledge

Phenomena: in Kantian terms, the world of everyday things that we can detect with our senses

Things to remember

▶ Nietzsche's interest in philosophy was initially inspired by reading Schopenhauer, who had an influence on his doctrine of the will to power.

▶ Nietzsche was good friends with the German composer Richard Wagner, who proved to be a huge influence on his early writings.

▶ *The Death of Tragedy* (1871) is the work that shows the most intense influence of Wagner on Nietzsche's ideas. Thereafter, Wagner's influence waned as Nietzsche grew disillusioned with both his ideas (including his anti-Semitism) and the man himself.

▶ Other philosophers who influenced Nietzsche were Plato, Descartes, Locke, Berkeley, Hume and Kant, although he contested many of their ideas.

▶ Like Schopenhauer, Nietzsche developed a poetic style of writing philosophy that was very different from the dry academic tone adopted by most of his contemporaries.

Fact-check

1 Who was the greatest influence on Nietzsche's first major work *The Birth of Tragedy*?
  a Plato
  b Kant
  c Schopenhauer
  d Wagner

2 Which *one* of the following is *not* a Wagner opera?
  a *Tannhauser*
  b *Lohengrin*
  c *Romeo and Juliet*
  d *Tristan and Isolde*

3 Which small town premiered Wagner's *Ring Cycle*?
  a Bath
  b Bayreuth
  c Berlin
  d Brighton

4 Which one of the following was an ancient Greek philosopher?
  a Locke
  b Spinoza
  c Plato
  d Descartes

5 What is empiricism?
  a The philosophical position that we can acquire knowledge of the world through direct experience of the senses
  b The philosophical position that reason, the intellect, forms the basis for much of our knowledge
  c The philosophical position that there are two worlds: the physical and the non-physical
  d The philosophical position that there is only the mind, no external world

6 What is rationalism?

   a The philosophical position that we can acquire knowledge of the world through direct experience of the senses

   b The philosophical position that reason, the intellect, forms the basis for much of our knowledge

   c The philosophical position that there are two worlds: the physical and the non-physical

   d The philosophical position that there is only the mind, no external world

7 What is idealism?

   a The philosophical position that we can acquire knowledge of the world through direct experience of the senses

   b The philosophical position that reason, the intellect, forms the basis for much of our knowledge

   c The philosophical position that there are two worlds: the physical and the non-physical

   d The philosophical position that there is only the mind, no external world

8 What is dualism?

   a The philosophical position that we can acquire knowledge of the world through direct experience of the senses

   b The philosophical position that reason, the intellect, forms the basis for much of our knowledge

   c The philosophical position that there are two worlds: the physical and the non-physical

   d The philosophical position that there is only the mind, no external world

9 What, for Kant, is meant by 'noumena'?

   a The world of everyday things that we can detect with our sense

   b Metaphysical beliefs about the soul, the cosmos and God, which are matters of faith rather than scientific, empirical knowledge

   c There is only the mind, no external world

   d There is only the external world, no mind

10 What, for Kant, is meant by 'phenomena'?
   a The world of everyday things that we can detect with our senses
   b Metaphysical beliefs about the soul, the cosmos and God, which are matters of faith rather than scientific, empirical knowledge
   c That there is only the mind, no external world
   d That there is only the external world, no mind

Dig deeper

Christopher Janaway, *Schopenhauer: A Very Short Introduction* (Oxford: OUP, 2002)

Bryan Magee, *The Philosophy of Schopenhauer* (Oxford: Clarendon Press, 1997)

Bryan Magee, *Wagner and Philosophy* (London: Penguin, 2001)

Arthur Schopenhauer, *Essays and Aphorisms* (London: Penguin, 2004)

Arthur Schopenhauer, *The World as Will and Representation*, 2 vols (New York: Dover Publications, 1966)

Twenty Minutes (30/08/13), BBC Radio 3: www.bbc.co.uk/programmes/

3

Nietzsche's later life and death

In this chapter you will learn:

▶ *about Nietzsche's friends*
▶ *about his retirement from teaching and his subsequent 'wanderings' and writing*
▶ *about his relationships with Lou Salomé and Paul Rée*
▶ *about his final years*
▶ *about his sister Elisabeth.*

Throughout much of his mature life Nietzsche was godless, stateless, homeless and wifeless. Ill health drove him to leave Basel in 1872 and go south to Italy, and he spent the next ten years wandering in Europe. Despite his illness, Nietzsche now started to produce his greatest, most mature works. These included *Dawn* (1881), which attacks the idea that morality has any objective basis, *The Gay Science* (1882), which first declares the death of God, and *Thus Spoke Zarathustra* (1885), which talks of the 'Superman'. Perhaps above all, in his *Beyond Good and Evil* (1886) Nietzsche brings together all of his philosophy in the most systematic way. Nevertheless, he remained largely unknown and unread.

This chapter outlines the events of this period, his friendships with Malwida von Meysenbug, Paul Rée and Lou von Salomé, among others, and the development of his ideas before his decline into madness and death at the age of 54. It also examines the negative effect of his sister Elisabeth on his reputation.

Malwida von Meysenbug and Paul Rée

When Nietzsche was at Bayreuth in 1872, Cosima Wagner introduced him to a good friend of the Wagners and a Schopenhauer advocate, Malwida von Meysenbug (1816–1903). Meysenbug was a fascinating character in her own right and her *Memoirs of an Idealist* are worth reading. She was a campaigner for democracy and womens' rights and had fought for political reform in Germany in 1848, resulting in a decade of exile in England. When Meysenbug heard about Nietzsche's ill health, she recommended that he spend some time in Italy, and so he took a year's leave of absence from Basel starting in the autumn of 1876. No doubt Nietzsche had been considering for some time resigning his post as professor of philology and becoming a 'free philosopher' – a stateless and wandering exile. As someone who knew his Latin and Greek from stuffy libraries, the desire to 'go south' must have been great. He didn't go alone, however, but was accompanied by his friend the philosopher Paul Rée (1849–1901) and a 21-year-old Basel law student named Albert Brenner (1856–78).

Meysenbug considered herself something of a mentor for young German writers and artists. Nietzsche, Rée and Brenner joined her in the Villa Rubinacci, which had views over the sea to Naples and Vesuvius. Today, Villa Rubinacci is the name of the restaurant on Via Correale; the actual villa Nietzsche stayed in is next door and is now known as the Hotel Eden. Back then, the villa was located in a vineyard and catered for German visitors, and the three men had rooms on the first floor. At first, Nietzsche was uncomfortable, as Wagner had also decided to visit Italy and was staying at a hotel nearby. Nietzsche met up with Wagner a few times and such visits were cordial enough, but hardly inspiring. By this time, Wagner was a much older man (he was now 63) in Nietzsche's eyes and Nietzsche had outgrown him. Once Wagner left Italy, Nietzsche seemed to settle much better.

Nietzsche first met Rée in 1873 when the latter, though not a student, attended a series of lectures given by Nietzsche on the pre-Platonic philosophers. Rée was five years younger than Nietzsche and, by all accounts, much more precocious. The son of a Jewish landowner, Rée was also an atheist, but his view of existence as having no ultimate meaning led him into pessimism, whereas it tended to liberate Nietzsche. Originally, Rée had been a law student but became attracted to philosophy, and he was also interested in the importance of psychology as a way of understanding the beliefs of human beings. More specifically, Rée was interested in religious and moral beliefs, explaining religious experience as an attempt to interpret the world rather than as witness to an objective reality. Nietzsche was particularly influenced, however, by what Rée had to say about morality.

Nietzsche saw the villa as a 'monastery for free spirits' and later wrote, 'In Sorrento I shook off nine years of moss.' The three 'free sprits' worked on their books and they read (usually Rée would read aloud to Nietzsche) the works of the French moralists such as Montaigne, La Rochefoucauld and Vauvenargues. Inspired by Rée and these French thinkers, Nietzsche wrote aphorisms that were brought together and published as *Human, All Too Human* (1878) and *Dawn* (1881), also known as *Daybreak*. Rée, for his part, wrote *The Origin of the Moral Sensations*, a theme that has resonance in much of Nietzsche's own writing from this time on.

The visit to Sorrento was undoubtedly a turning point for Nietzsche, as it reinforced his decision to give up his professorial post and become a 'free spirit'. He was also set on finding himself a wife at this time and discussed this with Meysenbug. A letter he wrote to his sister Elisabeth on the topic while still in Sorrento is worth quoting:

> *'We [Nietzsche and Meysenbug] are convinced that in the long run I shall have to give up my Basel university life, that if I continued there it would be at the cost of all my more important designs and would involve a complete breakdown of my health. Naturally I shall have to remain there during next winter, but I shall finish with it at Easter 1878, provided we bring off the other arrangement, i.e. marriage with a suitable and necessarily well-to-do-woman. "Good but rich" as Frl. von M. [Meysenbug] says... This project will be pushed ahead this summer, in Switzerland, so that I should come back to Basel already married. Various persons have been invited to come to Switzerland, among them several names that will be quite unfamiliar to you...'*
>
> Friedrich Nietzsche, *Conversations with Nietzsche*, trans. by David J. Parent (Oxford: OUP, 1991), p. 109

Case study: Nietzsche's 'monastery'

Nietzsche, in line with how he perceived the ancient Greeks and the original purpose of philosophy, believed that his writings were not intended to be mere expositions of a philosophical point of view, but transforming, consciousness-raising exercises. He believed that those who read his books could be seduced into a new way of life, forming a counterculture to what was currently on offer. In practical terms, it was Nietzsche's ambition to set up a commune of free (though like-minded) thinkers, or what he called a 'monastery for free spirits'. His life with Malwida, Rée and Brenner was, he believed, the start of this monastery, and it is view that Malwida, at least, shared, for she saw this 'ideal family' as 'a kind of mission house for adults of both sexes to have a free development of the noblest spiritual life so that they could go forth into the world to sow the seeds of a new spiritualized culture' (C.P. Janz, *Friedrich Nietzsche: Biographie* (Munich-Vienna: Hanser, 1978), p. 750).

Nietzsche's 'monastery' was to be a 'new Greek academy' (G. Coli and M. Montinari (eds), *Nietzsche Briefwechsel: Kritische Gesamtausgabe* (Berlin: de Gruyter, 1975–2004), 11.5, 113), an educational institution of people who effectively 'dropped out' of society and, much like a religious monastery, would retreat from the day-to-day concerns of the world. Similarly, they would lead a simple, ascetic existence, rejecting materialism, instead engaging in studying, debating, and creating works of art, literature, philosophy and science. While retreating from the concerns of humankind, the ultimate aim – like Nietzsche's Zarathustra – was to return to humankind, to 'give back' what had been learned to redeem civilization by presenting to the world a role model for another way of life.

Nietzsche never actually carried out his 'project', but he became more convinced of one thing – to end his academic career, especially as his health continued to deteriorate. In April 1879 he suffered from a bout of disabling headaches, which exhausted him completely. Consequently, he asked to be relieved of his teaching and, in June, he was retired on a small but manageable (given his meager requirements) pension.

Nietzsche's wanderings

'I am a wanderer and a mountain-climber (he said to his heart), I do not like the plains and it seems I cannot sit still for long. And whatever may yet come to me as fate and experience – a wandering and a mountain climbing will be in it: in the final analysis one only experiences oneself.'
Thus Spake Zarathustra, Part Three, 'The Wanderer'

In *Beyond Good and Evil*, perhaps his greatest book, Nietzsche calls for the coming of a 'new philosopher', or 'free spirits' as he calls them. In looking at Nietzsche's life, his 'wanderings', we can understand better what Nietzsche meant by these new philosophers. For the next ten years (1879–89), Nietzsche, with only the clothes on his back and a trunkful of possessions, wandered through Italy, southern France and Switzerland. He had been advised by the doctor to seek more clement environments for his health, and this he attempted to do.

Nietzsche's 'wanderings' should not be seen as periods of isolation and solitude. He was not leading a hermit existence like Zarathustra in his ten-year retreat to the mountains. Nietzsche continued to have close friends and even, perhaps, a lover for a brief time, during his ten-year spell. He could probably have ended a life of relative solitude had he so wished, but he did not wish it; periods of solitude probably suited his nature. There were times of melancholy and regret and, while he continued to have friends, undoubtedly these friends began to feel that Nietzsche was testing their friendship to the limit. As his friends got older, their responsibilities to family and other things took over, and they had less time for the wandering idealist, however charismatic that figure may have been.

One such friend was Peter Gast. Gast's real name was Heinrich Köselitz, but he adopted the name of Gast when he began to work seriously as a composer. In 1875 Gast, seven years younger than Nietzsche, went to Basel to study and became something of Nietzsche's 'disciple'. He first became Nietzsche's secretary, writing down his work as Nietzsche dictated, but later it seems that Gast was actually in love with Nietzsche, if Gast's letters to a friend from 1879 to 1881 are anything to go by: 'I have never loved a man as I do him, not even my father...'

In 1880, for the sake of his health, Nietzsche travelled to Riva at Lake Garda. Gast was nearby in Venice, struggling to gain recognition as a composer, but when Nietzsche told him he was at Riva, Gast packed his bags and joined him. Gast's letters tell us that this proved to be a trying and miserable time. The weather in Riva was bad, which prompted Gast to write to a friend:

Spotlight

Nietzsche took advantage of Gast's love for him, which pushed even his greatest disciple to his limits:

'You have no idea what I endured... how many a night I lay down and tried to sleep and when I thought about what had happened during the day, and saw that I had done nothing for myself and everything for other people, I was often seized with such rage that I threw myself into contortions and called down death and damnation on Nietzsche. I have hardly ever felt so bad as I did during this time... Then, when I had at last managed to go to sleep at four or five in the morning, Nietzsche would often come along at nine or ten and ask if I would play Chopin for him.'
Peter Gast, quoted in R.J. Hollingdale, *Nietzsche: The Man and His Philosophy* (Cambridge: CUP, 2001), p. 127

The writing of *Dawn*

Nietzsche spent the winter of 1880–81 in Genoa, finishing his work on *Dawn*. He then approached his old friend Carl van Gersdorff with a proposal to travel together to Tunis. Gersdorff had first met Nietzsche in 1863 when the former – then a student himself – had read an essay Nietzsche had written and was so impressed that he made a point of meeting him. Gersdorff, probably under the influence of Nietzsche, became a 'Schopenhauerian', as well as part of the Wagner entourage. Gersdorff and Nietzsche would spend holidays together, and Gersdorff also attended some of Nietzsche's lectures along with Paul Rée. However, when Nietzsche suggested that he and Gersdorff spend a couple of years in Tunis together, the latter was reluctant, and Nietzsche himself changed his mind when war broke out there. Nietzsche then considered travelling to Mexico, but this idea never came to fruition.

During this time Nietzsche was particularly excited over his new work *Dawn*, declaring that, 'This is the book with which people are likely to associate my name' and '…I have produced one of the boldest and most sublime and most thought-provoking books ever born out of the human brain and heart.' But curiously, only two months after giving *Dawn* such praise, he wrote to Rée describing the book as 'poor piecemeal philosophy'. What had taken place to make Nietzsche change his mind? An interesting experience occurred while Nietzsche was staying in Sils-Maria in the Upper Engadine mountains of Switzerland, which Nietzsche himself described:

'I shall now tell the story of Zarathustra. The basic conception of the work, the idea of eternal recurrence, the highest formula of affirmation that can possibly be attained – belong to the August of the year 1881: it was jotted down on a piece of paper with the inscription: "6,000 feet beyond man and time". I was that day walking through the woods beside the lake of Silvaplana; I stopped beside a mighty pyramidal block of stone which reared itself up not far from Surlei. Then this idea came to me.'

Ecce Homo, Thus Spoke Zarathustra I

This 'idea' of the eternal recurrence (see Chapter 7) is described in a way that suggests an almost religious experience that Nietzsche had. In fact, in *Ecce Homo* he elaborates more on this 'vision' which he calls an 'inspiration':

'If one had the slightest residue of superstition left in one, one would hardly be able to set aside the idea that one is merely incarnation, merely mouthpiece, merely medium of overwhelming forces. The concept of revelation, in the sense that something suddenly, with unspeakable certainty and subtlety, becomes visible, audible, simply describes the fact. One hears, one does not seek; one takes, one does not ask who gives; a thought flashes up like lightning, with necessity, unfalteringly formed – I have never had any choice. An ecstasy whose tremendous tension sometimes discharges itself in a

This 'inspiration' is not conceived of in terms of ideas that Nietzsche himself invented, but rather it comes across as a mystical feeling 'of power, of divinity'. In the same book, when Nietzsche talks of his 'conception' of Zarathustra, he says, 'It was on these two walks that the whole of the first Zarathustra came to me, above all Zarathustra himself, as a type: more accurately, he stole up on me…'

Nietzsche described this experience in a letter to his friend Peter Gast, written in August 1881. He described his elation, and his tears: 'Not sentimental tears, mind you, but tears of joy, to the accompaniment of which I sang and talked nonsense, filled with a new vision far superior to that of other men.'

This experience is certainly significant, and any student of Nietzsche should be hesitant in describing him as lacking a spiritual side. Nietzsche's experience beside the lake of Silvaplana tells us much about Nietzsche's religiosity. He could hardly be described as a rationalist, and even the term 'empiricist' is not entirely accurate. In fact, he often comes across as a philosophical Romantic. Some have suggested that this experience is the first sign of Nietzsche's madness, but to suggest this is to discount all of his writings after *Dawn* as the product of a madman when, in fact, he goes on to produce much more mature and philosophically rigorous work than previously. What the Surlej experience does tell us, however, is that Nietzsche saw himself as entering a new phase in his philosophical enterprise, a belief that he now had a 'calling', for want of a better term, that would lead to *Thus Spoke Zarathustra*. In this sense, we can say that Nietzsche looked to his earlier works as 'piecemeal philosophy'.

Lou von Salomé

From 1882 Nietzsche's thoughts were already on *Zarathustra*, with Part One written by February 1883. Paul Rée had spent some time with Nietzsche in Genoa before heading off to Rome in March 1882. At the same time, Nietzsche, curiously, headed to Messina in Sicily. Usually, at that time of year, Nietzsche would have headed for more northerly climes. Whatever the reason, he seemed happy enough there. He wrote to Gast:

> *'So, I have arrived at "my corner of the earth", where, according to Homer, happiness is said to dwell. Truly, I have never been in such good spirits as in the past week, and my fellow citizens are pampering and spoiling me in the most charming way.'*
> Nietzsche, quoted in Roger Safranski, *Nietzsche: A Philosophical Biography* (London: Granta, 2003), p. 244

Spotlight

Writers have often speculated about Nietzsche's sexuality, suggesting that his pragmatic approach to marriage fit with homosexual tendencies. His unconventional visit to Messina has been seen as an attempt to fulfil his homoerotic fantasies, as Messina at the time was home to a homosexual colony. Such speculation, however, must remain just that, unless further evidence comes to light.

Rée, for his part, stayed at Malwida von Meysenbug's house in Rome. There he met the 20-year-old Lou von Salomé (1861–1937) and immediately fell in love with her. Born in St Petersburg and the daughter of a Russian general of Huguenot descent, Salomé had left Russia with her mother in 1880 to study at the University of Zurich. She had developed a severe lung disease and her doctors, who gave her only a few years to live, suggested she head south in search of a better climate to aid her recovery, which was how she came to be staying in Meysenbug's house.

No doubt her feeling that she would not live long gave Salomé an extra passion for life and an enthusiasm for the study of philosophy that would have attracted many to her. It certainly had an effect on Rée, and they would walk the streets of Rome night after night discussing their ideas. Rée wrote excitedly to Nietzsche about Salomé, and one response from Nietzsche is particularly interesting:

> 'Give that Russian girl my regards if that makes any sense: I lust after this kind of soul. Indeed, I plan to go on the prowl for one quite soon; considering what I wish to accomplish in the next ten years, I need one. Marriage is an altogether different story – I could agree only to a maximum of two years of marriage.'
>
> Nietzsche, quoted in Roger Safranski, *Nietzsche: A Philosophical Biography* (London: Granta, 2003), p. 250

Spotlight

Nietzsche's attitude to marriage seems to have been purely pragmatic: it was a case of needing someone to run the household and, more importantly, to act as his amanuensis. Previously, he had relied upon his friends for this and, apparently, had also acquired a typewriter about which he complained bitterly as being defective, although it is hard to imagine Nietzsche – with his severe migraines – banging away at a typewriter. It would have made an interesting thesis to investigate whether Nietzsche's style altered as a result of using a typewriter, but, alas, no typewritten manuscripts of his seem to exist – and so he probably never used it at all.

Nietzsche certainly seemed to lack certain social skills when it came to marriage proposals. In April 1876 he had proposed marriage to a woman he hardly knew, having met her only three times. He was promptly rejected, but this did not seem to bother Nietzsche very much. When, after having spent three weeks in Messina, he turned up in Rome in April 1882 it was only a matter of days before he proposed to Salomé. Rée had also proposed to Salomé, but her response to both of them was that she was not interested in marriage, but would rather form a kind of intellectual *ménage à trois,* in which the three of them would share an apartment in Vienna or Paris, writing, studying and debating. This idea certainly seemed to appeal to Nietzsche; it fit with his dream of a 'secular monastery'.

Such a threesome was bound to fail eventually, given the egos and competitive nature of the three characters. But the *ménage à trois* did not occur immediately. First, Salomé spent some time with Rée and his mother in West Prussia and then, in August, she spent three weeks in Tautenburg with Nietzsche and his sister Elisabeth. Nietzsche's sister took a dislike to Salomé and considered the idea of such a threesome insane. At Tautenburg, Salomé and Nietzsche were housed in separate apartments and they would take long walks together. While she loved the conversations, she did not love Nietzsche:

> *'In some deep dark corner of our beings we are worlds apart. Nietzsche's nature is like an old castle that conceals within it many a dark dungeon and hidden basement room, not apparent at first glance and yet likely to contain all the essentials. It is strange, but recently the idea suddenly struck me that we could wind up facing each other as enemies someday.'*
> Lou Salomé, quoted in Roger Safranski, *Nietzsche: A Philosophical Biography* (London: Granta, 2003), p.254

Salomé's prediction was later to prove correct, as evidenced from a letter Nietzsche wrote (but never sent) to Paul Rée's brother, in July 1883: 'This scrawny dirty smelly monkey with her fake breasts – a disaster!'

In the meantime, however, plans were drawn to set up the *ménage à trois* in Paris, and Nietzsche began to make inquiries among many of his friends in Paris regarding accommodation. However, he had not realized that by this time Rée was becoming increasingly jealous of Nietzsche in the relationship. He thought that Nietzsche presented a possible threat to his own romantic intentions towards Salomé, and so he arranged for himself and Salomé to live far away from Nietzsche, in Berlin. Nietzsche was never to see either of them again.

The final years

Undoubtedly, the realization that he had been ditched, that he had been taken in by a 21-year-old, had an emotional effect upon Nietzsche. For solace, he now buried himself in his work *Thus Spoke Zarathustra*. Reading the opening pages of *Zarathustra,* we can see this as autobiographical, as it paints a picture of the suffering and solitude that Nietzsche himself now felt. *Thus Spoke Zarathustra* also helps us understand what Nietzsche means by the 'new philosophers'. There has been much debate as to what these philosophers would be like, what they would do, what morality they would possess, and so on. To understand this, you need to understand Nietzsche's own life and how this is partly autobiographical through his character of Zarathustra.

Nietzsche felt alone in the world. For company, he turned to his sister, who made every effort to ruin the name of Salomé by writing letters decrying her character and her 'immoral' lifestyle with Rée. Nietzsche, it seemed, may well have been party to this dung throwing.

The year 1888 was the last of Nietzsche's sane life, although it was also the start of his fame. He spent the beginning of that fateful year in Nice, stayed in Turin from April till June, spent the summer in Sils-Maria, and then returned to Turin in September. It was, in this respect, a year of his usual wanderings, but in other respects it was very different. In his correspondence, Nietzsche reported that his health was improving and that he felt a sense of joy and elation with life, not recognizing that these feelings of euphoria were symptomatic of forthcoming megalomania.

Added to this tragedy of oncoming madness was the fact that Nietzsche was never to appreciate the success and influence his work was to have, for undoubtedly he courted notoriety and wanted success. It was on the very first day of 1888 that the first ever review of Nietzsche's whole work appeared in a German newspaper. A few months later, in April, the internationally renowned Danish critic and biographer Georg Brandes (1842–1927) gave a series of popular lectures on Nietzsche at Copenhagen University. Nietzsche had finally arrived, yet his letters were becoming more and more bizarre, evidence of his looming mental breakdown.

In this final year of sanity, Nietzsche was as prolific a writer as ever. He wrote six short books: *The Wagner Case*, *The Twilight of the Idols*, *The Anti-Christ*, *Ecce Homo*, *Nietzsche contra Wagner* and *Dithyrambs of Dionysus*. Are these works in any way a reflection of Nietzsche's approaching insanity? They do not introduce any new philosophy, nor do they contradict what he had previously said. There is evident continuation from his previous work, and the structure is generally tight and presented in a magnificent poetic style. These works deserve attention, therefore, and show no evidence of Nietzsche having lost his intellectual capacity – quite the contrary.

DESCENT INTO INSANITY

On 3 January 1889, according to a well-known although possibly apocryphal account, Nietzsche walked out of his lodgings and saw in the piazza a cabman beating his horse. Nietzsche cried out, ran across the square and threw his arms around the neck of the horse. At that moment he lost consciousness. A crowd gathered and the landlord of Nietzsche's lodgings carried the still-unconscious Nietzsche back to his room. When he finally came to, he shouted, sang and punched away at the piano. Once he had calmed down, he wrote a series of epistles to his friends and the courts of Europe declaring that he, signed 'the Crucified', would be going to Rome in five days' time and that all the princes of Europe and the Pope should assemble.

Nietzsche, at the age of 44, was now permanently insane. One of his few remaining friends, Overbeck, disturbed by the letters, went to Turin and persuaded Nietzsche to travel to Basel with him and enter the mental asylum there. From here, he was transferred to a clinic in Jena, near his mother's home. At the clinic, Nietzsche behaved like an imperious ruler, surveying the premises as if they were his palace. His conversation would switch from the rational to the nonsensical and violent at any given moment. When it was clear that no improvement was possible, his mother took him home with her to Naumburg. She looked after him devotedly for seven years, watching him fall steadily into decline and apathy. After his mother's death in 1897, the care of Nietzsche until his own death in 1900 was left in the hands of his sister Elisabeth.

Elisabeth Förster-Nietzsche

Much of Nietzsche's legacy is closely related to his sister's less
favourable legacy. Elisabeth Nietzsche (1846–1935), more than
any other person, is responsible for the misunderstandings that
have accompanied Nietzsche's philosophy to this day. When
Nietzsche started writing poetry at the age of eight, it was the
six-year-old Elisabeth who collated them for him. At such an
early age, she already felt responsible for the work and life of
the shy Friedrich.

Elisabeth loved the first Bayreuth Festival in 1876 – the event
that Nietzsche hated so much. She had already got to know
Wagner through her brother and she was captivated by the
composer's anti-Semitic ideas. At the festival, she met and fell in
love with Bernhard Förster, an anti-Semitic fanatic who was also
attracted to Wagner's writings on Jews. Förster saw in Wagner
a guide who would help him to become a professional anti-
Semite, a member of the notorious 'German Seven' who called
for the registration of Jews and the stop on Jewish immigration.
Much to the disgust of Nietzsche, Förster married Elisabeth,
who, for her part, attempted unsuccessfully to recruit her
brother into the anti-Semitic cause.

Wagner once wrote of the possibility of establishing a pure
German colony in South America where Jews would be banned.
Even though Wagner himself knew little about South America,
Bernhard Förster took up his idea with great enthusiasm. He
formed a group of somewhat disparate disciples and they,
together with Elisabeth, sailed off to Paraguay, where they
established a colony called Nueva Germania in 1887. The
colony did not thrive, however, and although it still exists today,
it has integrated with the Paraguayan culture and people.

As for Bernhard Förster, he grew increasingly in debt and
committed suicide in the same year that Nietzsche went mad.

Nietzsche's madness was the excuse Elisabeth needed to abandon Nueva Germania to its fate, and pursue her new full-time mission of making her brother famous. For the next 40 years, Elisabeth manipulated his works and superimposed her own racist views upon them.

THE NIETZSCHE ARCHIVE

On returning to Germany, Elisabeth – who represented everything that Nietzsche hated about Germany and Germans – became his guardian and owner of his copyrights. Immediately, Elisabeth set about taking control of all of Nietzsche's writings. When Nietzsche collapsed in madness, he left behind mounds of unpublished material at his various lodgings. Elisabeth established an archive in a house in Naumburg that would become a museum of Nietzsche's works. As well as his works, however, Nietzsche himself was lodged in a room as one of the exhibits. Incapable of coherent speech, he was exhibited to important visitors and dressed in a white robe like a Brahman priest. Elisabeth turned her brother into a prophet, surrounding him in mystique and turning his madness into something seemingly superhuman.

The collected works of Nietzsche brought Elisabeth fame and fortune, and she became the official mouthpiece for her brother. However, in collecting his works, she would ignore any of his philosophy that she did not agree with, forge letters that she claimed Nietzsche had written to her that praised her, and wrote a popular biography of Nietzsche that was full of lies. The greatest sin of all was that she collected Nietzsche's unpublished notes into a book called *The Will to Power*. She claimed that this was Nietzsche's final testament, his true philosophy, whereas it is full of discarded thoughts and poorly written notes that Nietzsche had no intention of publishing. Although of historical interest, it is a shame that it is still quoted as an authority of Nietzsche's philosophy. Nietzsche's unpublished notes can be very helpful in understanding Nietzsche's thought processes, but they do need to be treated for what they are.

Nietzsche, at a time before his mental collapse and the falling out with his sister, had once written to Elisabeth requesting that, at his death – for he always believed he would die young – he should be given a pagan burial, with no priest at his grave. However, when he died on 25 August 1900, Elisabeth gave him a full Lutheran funeral and buried him in a coffin with a silver cross.

Key ideas

Philosophical Romanticism: The Romantic Movement was at its height in most of Europe during the first half of the nineteenth century. It affected most aspects of intellectual and cultural life. In philosophy, it is perhaps best understood as not being a complete rejection of empiricism, but rather also emphasizing the importance of nature, the emotions, and so on, in an understanding of what it means to be human

Anti-Semitism: A form of racism, prevalent during Nietzsche's time, that focused on prejudice against and hatred towards Jewish religion and/or ethnicity

Nazism: The fascist, anti-Semitic ideology of the twentieth-century political party – founded by Adolf Hitler – *Nationalsozialistische Deutsche Arbeiterpartei*, or Nazi Party.

Eternal recurrence: The idea that time is cyclical rather than linear, and that the universe will recur an infinite number of times

Zarathustra: A Persian prophet also known as Zoroaster and the founder of the religion of Zoroastrianism. Nietzsche took the name for a 'new prophet' who would turn morality on its head

Things to remember

▶ Nietzsche's severe, debilitating headaches grew worse to the extent that he had to give up his academic career in 1879.

▶ Nietzsche spent the next ten years (1879–89) wandering in various countries for the sake of his health. These proved to be very productive years in terms of his writing.

▶ In August 1881 Nietzsche had the 'inspiration' for *Zarathustra* while walking through the woods beside the lake of Silvaplana in Switzerland.

▶ By 1885 Nietzsche had completed *Thus Spoke Zarathustra*, followed by *Beyond Good and Evil* the next year.

▶ The year 1888 was the last of Nietzsche's sane life, although it was also the year when he started to receive recognition.

▶ Nietzsche spent his final years (1889–1900) insane, cared for by his mother and then his sister Elisabeth.

▶ Elisabeth Förster- Nietzsche, an anti-Semite, edited Nietzsche's works and later presented him, falsely, as the 'Nazi philosopher'.

▶ Nietzsche died on 25 August 1900 and was given a Christian burial, against his own wishes.

Fact-check

1 What was Nietzsche's 'monastery for free spirits'?
   a A place where people could drink alcohol for free
   b A nudist colony
   c A place to read, study and debate
   d A place of worship and prayer

2 Why did Nietzsche retire from his professorship?
   a Because of disabling headaches
   b He inherited a fortune
   c He was fired from his post
   d He married a millionaire

3 Which one of the following is not a book by Nietzsche?
   a *Dawn*
   b *Midnight*
   c *The Gay Science*
   d *Human, All Too Human*

4 What was the name of Nietzsche's 'prophet' in his book of the same name?
   a Muhammad
   b Buddha
   c Zarathustra
   d Abraham

5 Which one of the following books did Nietzsche *not* write in his final year of sanity?
   a *Beyond Good and Evil*
   b *The Twilight of the Idols*
   c *The Anti-Christ*
   d *Ecce Homo*

6 In which year did Nietzsche have his mental breakdown?
   a 1900
   b 1888
   c 1889
   d 1898

7 Where did Nietzsche's sister and her husband set up a new German colony?

  a Paraguay

  b Uruguay

  c Peru

  d Argentina

8 What was the name of the compilation of Nietzsche's unpublished notes?

  a *Ecce Homo*

  b *The Will to Power*

  c *The Eternal Recurrence*

  d *Untimely Meditations*

9 In which year did Nietzsche die?

  a 1890

  b 1900

  c 1914

  d 1899

10 What kind of funeral did Nietzsche receive?

  a A pagan burial

  b Burial at sea

  c A scattering of his ashes over his favourite mountains

  d A full Lutheran funeral

Dig deeper

Lindsey Chamberlain, *Nietzsche in Turin: An Intimate Biography* (London: Picador, 1999)

Friedrich Nietzsche, *Conversations with Nietzsche*, trans. by David J. Parent (Oxford: OUP, 1991)

Lance Olsen, *Nietzsche's Kisses: A Novel* (Salt Lake City: Fc2, 2006)

Roger Safranski, *Nietzsche: A Philosophical Biography* (London: Granta, 2003)

Lou Salomé, *Nietzsche* (Illinois: University of Illinois Press, 2001)

Robin Small, *Nietzsche and Rée: A Star Friendship* (Oxford: OUP, 2005)

Julia Vickers, *Lou von Salomé: A Biography of the Woman Who Inspired Freud, Nietzsche and Rilke* (Jefferson: McFarland, 2008)

Irvin Yalom, *When Nietzsche Wept* (London: Harper Perennial, 2011)

4

The Birth of Tragedy

In this chapter you will learn:

▶ *about the reception of Nietzsche's first major work* The Birth of Tragedy

▶ *about his teachings on Apollo and Dionysus*

▶ *about his criticisms of the 'theoretical man'.*

As he suggested, Nietzsche certainly was 'born posthumously' in the sense that his first major work, *The Birth of Tragedy*, fell upon deaf ears when it was first published, and yet is now considered to be an inspired account of Greek tragedy and is studied in many universities across the world. Despite Nietzsche's acknowledged brilliance and precociousness, this first work did not help to cement that reputation in academic circles; in fact, it did more harm than good and its publication was heavily criticized by scholars.

Although Nietzsche was himself later critical of *The Birth of Tragedy*, it is still an excellent read and many of the ideas contained within it crop up in Nietzsche's later writings. The book deserves a chapter of its own because the work itself stands out as a unique and interesting thesis.

The 'theoretical man'

Nietzsche's dissatisfaction with the academic world is reflected in *The Birth of Tragedy*. The young Ulrich von Wilamowitz-Möllendorf (1848–1931) was among the many scholars who attacked Nietzsche's book, writing a 32-page pamphlet with the sarcastic title *Philology of the Future*. Sarcastic maybe, but the point was made that Nietzsche was being far too ambitious and visionary, and lacked the limited – some would say 'dry' – pragmatism of academia. However, Nietzsche either refused or was unable to write within the accepted norms of the academic style, considering himself to be more of a poet. He saw his writing as an outlet for his artistic capabilities, and his early writing also shows the influence of his relationship with Wagner. Needless to say, Wagner considered *The Birth of Tragedy* a wonderful piece of work, but this is hardly surprising considering how much praise it heaps upon the composer.

A first impression of *The Birth of Tragedy* may make one wonder why Nietzsche chose to consider Greek tragedy, given his intention to produce a work that would have contemporary cultural significance, but this ignores the importance of Greek culture at the time. It was not, then, as many people today might see it (quite wrongly), a 'dead' subject with little importance except for those with the luxury to study it. While, on the one hand, there was a push towards industrialization and marketplace values, there was, on the other hand, an increasing disillusionment with the goals and values of modernity accompanied by a looking back to bygone eras, most notably that of ancient Greece. It was felt by many, poets and artists chief among them, that the Greeks possessed a set of values, a spirituality and an affirmation of life that seemed to be desperately lacking among industrialized, scientific, modern humanity. This condemnation of modernity was something Nietzsche shared. The following passage from *The Birth of Tragedy* is particularly enlightening:

'Our whole modern world is caught in the net of Alexandrian culture, and the highest ideal it knows is theoretical man, equipped with the highest powers of understanding and working in the service of science, whose archetype and progenitor is Socrates. The original aim of all our means of education is to achieve this ideal; every other form of existence has to fight its way up alongside it, as something permitted but not intended.'

The Birth of Tragedy, 18

The 'theoretical man', the man of science and progress, is what Nietzsche consistently condemned throughout his writing career. This certainly reflects modern-day concerns where success is measured by how much money and property you possess rather than by, for want of a better word, your 'wisdom'.

Interestingly, Nietzsche presents Socrates as an example of this 'theoretical man'. In the philosophical realm, Socrates is considered one of the greatest philosophers, yet Nietzsche frequently criticizes him as the 'archetype' of those modern, alienating values. Little is known about the life of Socrates and, as he did not write anything down, we have to rely on the writings of his disciple Plato who used Socrates as his mouthpiece in his dialogues. Therefore, when Nietzsche talks of the philosophy of Socrates, he is not usually making any distinction from that of Plato.

Nietzsche disagreed with the following aspects of the philosophy of Socrates and Plato:

1 The Platonic view was that there is such a thing as objective truth. This view was a response to the belief in relativism: that morals and beliefs are a product of a particular time and place and that, therefore, there is no such thing as 'right' and 'wrong'.

2 Plato argued that the world we live in is essentially an illusion, a poor image of a better, perfect world. The role of the philosopher, therefore, was to seek out this better world rather than be preoccupied with everyday existence.

3 Plato believed that the true world could be accessed through the power of reason. Humankind has both instinct and the capacity to reason, but frequently prefers to follow instinct and ignore reason, just like other animals. Plato argues that, by exercising reason – the intellect – humankind can know what truth is.

Finally, Nietzsche lays the blame for over 2,000 years of this kind of philosophy and the death of tragedy at the foot of Socrates. In particular, Nietzsche considered the whole philosophical concern with metaphysics, the speculation on what exists beyond the physical world, to be an error and a distraction from what really mattered.

For Socrates, tragedy was no longer required because reason could remove the fear of death. Although Nietzsche admired the genius of Socrates, as well as his achievements, he saw Socrates as representative of the desire to explain, to engage in argument and counter-argument, rather than accept that ultimately there are no explanations. Also, Nietzsche was not against reason and science; he would be the first to praise its achievements and its role in the enhancement of life. What he condemned was the regard for reason as a provider of answers, delivering humankind from a state of ignorance.

Despite Nietzsche's solitude and bouts of depression, he always argued for an affirmation of life, of saying 'yes' to life, rather than adopting the resigned cynicism of, say,

Schopenhauer. This quality, he believed, existed among the ancient Greeks, although they had much to complain about given the harshness of existence for most of them, certainly in comparison to the luxury enjoyed by modern Europeans. Nietzsche talked often of the importance of 'health', especially in conjunction with southern climes. These themes can be traced right back to *The Birth of Tragedy*.

Spotlight

Given that today Nietzsche is recognized as one of the world's great philosophers, he nonetheless was never trained in philosophical method, nor did he have much knowledge of the history of philosophical thought, including Aristotelian thought, the medieval scholastics and the British empiricists.

When Nietzsche was only 23 he had written to a friend that he hoped one day to combine philology with music, to produce music written with words rather than with notes. To do this, he needed a theme, and that of Greek tragedy seemed to fit the bill perfectly. Before starting to write *The Birth of Tragedy*, he had already set his stage, having given two public lectures in 1870.

The first of these lectures, 'Greek Music Drama', which examined Dionysian festivals as the origin of tragedy, was well received and kept well within the framework of classical philology of the time, but Nietzsche wanted to be much more ambitious than that. The second lecture, 'Socrates and Tragedy', according to Nietzsche, 'aroused terror and misconceptions'. How, one wonders, could a public lecture 'arouse terror'? This lecture, in line with what he was intent on saying in *The Birth of Tragedy*, was Nietzsche's first public condemnation of the great Socrates. It focused on the Greek philosopher's emphasis on rationalism as leading to the death of tragedy and, in Nietzsche's eyes, of wisdom. This dialectical will to knowledge destroyed the life forces of myth, religion and art. In this lecture, Nietzsche also suggested the possibility of a rebirth of Greek tragedy, although he did not at this point mention Wagner as this possible saviour.

Spotlight

Nietzsche was by no means ignorant of how cruel and brutal the world could be. When he wrote his essay 'The Dionysian Worldview' in 1870, the Franco-Prussian War had just been declared. Rather than remain in his cloistered ivory tower, Nietzsche voluntarily enlisted as a medical orderly.

Cosima Wagner tried to discourage Nietzsche from joining the medical service, telling him that his lack of training would hinder rather than help the cause. She suggested that he would be a much more beneficial contributor by sending a hundred cigarettes to the front. However, Nietzsche did not take her advice and for a short time he did experience war at first hand. As a medical orderly, he witnessed scenes of appalling suffering and destruction. In a letter to Wagner, he gave a graphic account of travelling for three days and nights in a cattle truck with the wounded. As it turned out, however, he spent only two weeks on the battlefields before contracting dysentery and diphtheria.

Case study: The Franco-Prussian War

The effect of the Franco-Prussian War on Nietzsche's physical and mental state cannot be underestimated, despite the relatively short time he spent in the field of war. When war was declared on 19 July 1870, Nietzsche's initial reaction was one of horror that Europe had failed to behave in a civilized manner (if only he had known what even more terrible events were to occur in the twentieth century), coupled with a hope that a new Europe would emerge from the devastation that the war would inevitably bring. He anticipated a Europe with a new culture and an increase across the continent of his 'monasteries' of 'free spirits' (see Chapter 4). At first, Nietzsche remained in neutral Switzerland, but upon hearing news of German victories, he felt obliged to enlist on the Prussian side.

The causes of the Franco-Prussian War are complicated. Essentially, it was sparked by France's growing concern that Prussia was effectively building a European empire by striving towards German unification. At that time, 'Germany' as such did not exist as a nation state; what unified these separate nations was the German language. It was the most powerful of these states, Prussia – under Chancellor Otto von Bismarck – that wanted to create one nation, which the French felt would destabilize the European balance of power.

The war lasted only a little over five months, but it resulted in half a million military casualties and an unknown number of civilians killed or wounded. The French were confident of victory but the Germans proved to better organized and equipped, usually with the latest that technology had to offer, and the French surrendered when Paris fell on 28 January 1871.

Apollo and Dionysus

It has already been mentioned (see Chapter 2) that Wagner's writings had a huge influence on Nietzsche's early work. Wagner held that there is a dualism between, on the one hand, humankind and Nature and, on the other hand, Art and Nature. In *The Artwork of the Future,* he argued that humankind, by exercising its intellect, is actually being drawn away from Nature and, therefore, its true Art. The fulfilled person is one who is in touch with their true nature and can express this through the medium of the perfect Art. Here, Wagner is making parallels between the role and function of Art with religion. It is perhaps inevitable that, when Wagner talks of his own art as being the model for the perfect, then Wagner – as the composer for this art – must be a religious 'saviour'.

In *The Birth of Tragedy*, Nietzsche gave importance to Art as a medium through which we comprehend the world. He took on board this dualism of Art and Nature under the principles of Apollo and Dionysus. These two Greek gods are presented as a metaphor for two fundamental principles:

▶ **The Apollonian:** Nietzsche compares the Apollonian with dreams. In a dream, you express fantasies but these are a way of forgetting the world rather than confronting the realities of the world. Apollonian art is exemplified by painting and sculpture. In the same way that we conjure up images in dreams, we do the same in painting. But these paintings are only representations of the world; they are fantasies that allow us to turn our backs, at least for a while, from the world we live in. Apollo, then, is an artistic style: that of form and clarity, and so is also represented most commonly in sculpture and architecture.

▶ **The Dionysian:** Nietzsche compares Dionysian art with intoxication. Nietzsche did not necessarily mean alcoholic intoxication, but rather the kind of ecstasy that can also be caused by other means than alcohol, for example sexual intercourse, dancing or religious activities. Like the Apollonian, the Dionysian is a mechanism for fleeing from reality, but intoxication is not the same as fantasy. Dream fantasies are an individual and private experience when you turn away from the world. Dionysian intoxication, however, is not about forgetting the world but forgetting your self and experiencing more of a mystical communal union. Dionysian art is more akin to music and poetry. Nietzsche accepted that the distinction between painting and music was not always so clear. It is quite possible, for example, to have Dionysian painting, and Nietzsche was aware that music had Apollo as its patron god. The more important distinction is how one responds to the work of art rather than the work of art itself. Nietzsche sees Apollo as expressing individuality, whereas the Dionysian revels in music and dance and so breaks down the individual like some kind of Sufi *dhikr* (meditative dance).

A way of understanding what these Dionysian energies are like can be ascertained from the following:

'From all corners of the ancient world (leaving aside the modern one in this instance), from Rome to Babylon, we can demonstrate the existence of Dionysiac festivals of a type which, at best, stand in the same relation to the Greek festivals as the bearded satyr, whose name and attributes were borrowed from the goat, stands to Dionysus himself. Almost everywhere an excess of sexual indiscipline, which flooded in waves over all family life and its venerable statutes, lay at the heart of such festivals. Here the very wildest of nature's beasts

The Dionysiac energies, therefore, when unleashed, are
dangerous, grotesque, cruel, sexual and wild. It is the rule of the
jungle: eat or be eaten. In such a vision of a conflicting, violent
world, it is difficult to find meaning or value or beauty but, for
Nietzsche, this did not mean a path towards nihilism. Rather,
his 'affirmation' – like the Greeks' – is to revel in this energy. In
a Schopenhauerian sense, the Dionysian represents the primary,
cruel, creative and elemental life force that Schopenhauer refers
to as Will. This gives Nietzsche's work an almost metaphysical
dimension, as he pictures the world as consisting of this
underlying life force that is 'cultured' by societies attempting to
live within its violence, anarchy and indifference. Culture, then,
is when human beings build up a livable framework in which to
survive in what is, in essence, a hostile climate. Some cultures,
notably the ancient Greeks as far as Nietzsche was concerned,
do this better than others.

The importance of culture

The importance of culture is another theme that runs through
all of Nietzsche's works. As already mentioned, when Nietzsche
was at Basel in 1869 he became acquainted with the historian
Jakob Burckhardt ('friend' would be too strong a word in
this case, as Burckhardt for his part kept his distance), and
was influenced by his most famous work, *The Culture of the
Renaissance in Italy*, published in 1860. Burckhardt, also
something of a pessimistic Schopenhauerian, was particularly

interested in the history of culture, as opposed to military or political history, and he argued for three major forces of existence: state, religion and culture. For Nietzsche, culture (which in his case could well include religion) was the highest objective, more so than, say, economics or science.

Nietzsche stresses that Apollo and Dionysus are not opposites but that they work side by side. They complement each other and, therefore, the perfect Art (in the Wagnerian sense) is one that embodies both the Apollonian and the Dionysian. Like Wagner, Nietzsche saw this Art as existing in Greek tragedy. Nietzsche's most important contribution in *The Birth of Tragedy* is the attack on the then-prevalent view that life in ancient Greece was idyllic. Rather, Nietzsche argued, the Greek way of life was brutal, short and full of suffering. How did the Greeks cope with these facts of life? Art, through the fusion of the Apollonian and the Dionysian, was their mechanism for making life tolerable.

The Apollonian element was needed to create the illusion – the fantasy – that distracted them from the horrors of everyday life. If, Nietzsche argued, the Greeks were indeed as happy and sunny as pictured, there would be no need for Apollonian art, and yet there is plenty of evidence in Greek tragedy to show that the Greeks suffered immensely. In Greek tragedy, we are presented with the images of gods and men, of heroes and monsters, as a way of transforming their fear of such things, in the same way that dreams are projections of our own fears and doubts.

The role of the chorus

The Dionysian element in Greek tragedy is represented by the chorus. The chorus would narrate the story through song. The chorus acted as an artistic substitute for the Dionysian rites by allowing the audience to identify themselves with these singing, dancing characters and therefore participate within the tragedy themselves and not be mere spectators. This was therapeutic, allowing audiences to feel a sense of unity with their fellows, with the chorus, and with the drama of the tragedy as well as to feel godlike themselves.

Nietzsche's participation in the Franco-Prussian War, brief though it was, tells us something about him and his views on war at this early age. (The fact that Nietzsche often uses militaristic terms in his writing has served to hinder an understanding of his philosophy, while encouraging those who wish to interpret him as a philosopher of war and military conquest.) Nietzsche had initially hailed the Franco-Prussian War as a catalyst for the revival of culture. However, he was not being nationalistic in any way, for he later distanced himself from the war when he realized that its primary motive was often more in line with profit-making and state-making. Rather, he saw war as part of the inevitable ingredient of culture-making.

An interesting essay, originally intended to be part of *The Birth of Tragedy,* is 'The Greek State', which Nietzsche had had printed privately; he sent a copy to Cosima Wagner. More will be said of this essay when looking at Nietzsche's politics (see Chapter 10), but for now it is worth noting that in this short work he argues that the state emerges from attempts to subdue war within its own frontiers and rather directs it outwards. The formation and continued existence of states requires that there will always be wars between these states, but in the 'intervals' society has breathing space to produce 'the radiant blossoms of genius' of culture in 'the concentrated effect of that *bellum* [warfare], turned inward' ('The Greek State', 7, 344). Here, Nietzsche was influenced by Burckhardt, who had argued that culture arises from agony. Nietzsche developed this line of thinking in arguing that war was a necessity for culture to thrive in what he calls the association of 'battlefield and artwork' ('The Greek State', 7, 344).

Life is tragic, and in *The Birth of Tragedy* Nietzsche wrote a phrase that has often been quoted since: 'Existence and the world are eternally justified solely as an aesthetic phenomenon' (*BT,* 5). A moral point of view may well argue for democracy and the welfare state, for the greatest happiness for the greatest number, but an aesthetic point of view – which Nietzsche advocates – is not concerned with such 'levelling'. If we are looking for recurrent themes in Nietzsche, then undoubtedly a key theme is his criticism of modernity, of the way we are now. This criticism rests upon two key features of modernity. First, we have lost what he calls our 'metaphysical solace' when faced with the certainty of death. Second, we have killed myth. In this sense, Nietzsche does not come across at all as a post-modern existentialist, but more of a traditionalist calling out for traditional, indeed ancient, values. Nietzsche says that the modern man is a myth-less man; when, for example, we go to the theatre we can no longer experience the 'miracle' that, for children, is a matter of course (*BT*, 23). We have lost the magic – in particular of art – because we have become too critical when studying history. The modern man breaks things down (is 'deconstructive'), reduces everything, rather than sees things in a more holistic manner.

In the first essay of *Untimely Meditations* (1873), for example, Nietzsche is critical of the Hegelian David Strauss. This is because Strauss wrote a 'deconstructive' *Life of Jesus* in 1835–6. History, as Nietzsche points out in the second essay of his *Untimely Meditations*, is not to be understood as 'events in the past', but rather as 'representations of the past'. While history of the right sort is essential for life, history of the wrong sort kills life. By 'life', Nietzsche means the growth of a people, a community, a culture. The mistake Strauss made was to write the wrong kind of history, to deconstruct a monumental figure. Strauss, by attempting to present an objective, scientific history, kills history and kills religion by presenting it as false, crude, irrational and absurd. Life, for Nietzsche, is possible only if we have illusion; religion is alive only if we have illusion. There is a place for science – at times Nietzsche was very positive about scientific progress – and there is a place for religion, but there is no place for a science of religion. The term 'modernity' (or even 'post-modernity') is often used today to cover many things in many different fields. For Nietzsche, modern man symbolized something dull, mediocre and lacking in excitement, imagination and passion for life.

Spotlight

There's a wonderful remark from the character Bernard Nightingale in Tom Stoppard's play *Arcadia*. He says:

'Why does scientific progress matter more than personalities? ... Don't confuse progress with perfectibility. A great poet is always timely. A great philosopher is an urgent need. There's no rush for Isaac Newton. We were quite happy with Aristotle's cosmos. Personally, I preferred it. Fifty-five crystal spheres geared to God's crankshaft is my idea of a satisfying universe. I can't think of anything more trivial than the speed of light...'

Nietzsche, for sure, would have seconded this view.

The value of Greek tragedy

In seeking to understand Nietzsche, it helps to put him in historical perspective. He saw, in Europe in particular, a decline in religious belief, which was being replaced by little in the way of positive values. This is why, in *The Birth of Tragedy*, he feels the need to look for 'salvation' – through Art in particular.

Nietzsche portrayed Greek tragedy as an interactive, mystical and unifying experience that provided a therapeutic outlet for a people who were sensitive to the suffering and uncertainties of everyday life, and in which humankind is in tune with Nature. Man is no longer an artist but a work of art. Art possesses form and so by making life a work of art we give the world a form, a structure. For Nietzsche, the greatest tragedians were Sophocles and Aeschylus in the fifth century BCE. He saw Euripides, the other tragedian often associated with these two, as the enemy of great Art.

Nietzsche argued that Euripides rid Greek drama of the role of the chorus, of the Dionysian element. The chorus became less central to the drama and became a matter of mere convention. Euripides, Nietzsche believed, killed tragedy. Nietzsche characterizes Euripides as a rational man who could not understand the seemingly irrational function of the chorus. When Wagner wrote of humankind turning away from Art and towards philosophy, Nietzsche saw this as a movement away from the instinctual, natural element towards the distant, rational capacity. Socrates, like Euripides, emphasized the importance of reason in the belief that, through the power of reason, we can gain access to truth. Nietzsche always placed a greater emphasis on the irrational and the instinctual, and also believed that there is no such thing as 'truth'. Great art is no 'truer' than science or religion, but Nietzsche believed art could at least put people in touch with Nature and their fellow human beings. It is an acceptance that there is only this life and it is full of suffering, rather than a belief that there is a better, pain-free life.

What has this got to do with the modern European whom Nietzsche was addressing? Although the ancient Greeks suffered, the tragedy of Classical Athens, Nietzsche believed, presents a balanced picture of the world. While understanding that individuals inevitably suffer in this life, there is solace in being aware of the underlying energies that pervade the world. As mentioned, Nietzsche saw Socrates as the precursor of an alternative, disabling, vision of 'optimism': an over-rationalized, logical, scientific view of the world that represses the emotions, the human instincts. At this time – and remember that Nietzsche was only 28 – he saw *The Birth of Tragedy* as a manifesto for change, as a call for a revolution. While such rhetoric is rarely appropriate in an academic text, it was heartfelt, reflecting Nietzsche's frustration with what he increasingly saw as dusty academia. He was also still in the grip of Schopenhauer and Kant to a large extent, and saw their philosophical enterprises as a break away from Socratic 'optimism'. The resurrection of the Greek world view was also present, Nietzsche thought, in music:

'From the Dionysiac ground of the German spirit a power has risen up which has nothing in common with the original conditions of Socratic culture and which can neither be explained not excused by these conditions; rather, this culture feels it to be something terrifying and inexplicable, something overpowering and hostile,

> *namely German music, as we see it in the mighty, brilliant course it has run from Bach to Beethoven, from Beethoven to Wagner. What can the knowledge-lusting Socratism of today hope to do with this daemon as it emerges from unfathomable depths?'*
>
> The Birth of Tragedy, 19

At this point in Nietzsche's philosophical career, he was not only under the influence of Wagner but also still Schopenhauerian and Kantian in his outlook. To their credit, which Nietzsche acknowledges, both these philosophers shared in Nietzsche's own enterprise in putting limits to the perceived unbounded scope of the scientific enterprise. Reason alone could not, after all, provide all the answers. He believed that humankind had lost all sense of purpose and was clinging on to religious and philosophical views that were no longer credible. He called for a return to the principles of Greek tragedy and devotes the final third of the book to praise of Wagner as the new tragedian.

In this respect, the book failed. While academics attacked it severely, Wagnerians – perhaps not surprisingly – praised it. Nietzsche himself, in a later preface to the book added in 1886, described it as badly written and confused:

> *'I repeat: I find it an impossible book today. I declare that it is badly written, clumsy, embarrassing, with a rage for imagery and confused in its imagery, emotional, here and there sugary to the point of effeminacy, uneven in pace, lacking the will to logical cleanliness, very convinced and therefore too arrogant to prove its assertions, mistrustful even in the propriety of proving things [... and so on...].'*
>
> The Birth of Tragedy, 'An Attempt at Self-criticism'

However, perhaps Nietzsche is too severe a critic of his own work. It has elements of originality and, most importantly, it raises the question of the importance of Art in our understanding of the world and our place within it. Art, together with our instinctual side, can also provide us with insights that are not accessible through reason.

Key ideas

Apollonian: Nietzsche's characterization of the Greek god Apollo as symbolic of painting and sculpture

Dionysian: Nietzsche's characterization of the Greek god Dionysus as symbolic of ecstatic music and dance and representative of the life force of the universe

Metaphysics: the speculation on what exists beyond the physical world, such as the existence of God and what is real

Modernity: a term with many meanings, but generally a reference to the increase in secularization accompanied by a belief in scientific progress

Relativism: the idea that morals and beliefs are a product of a particular time and place and that, therefore, there is no such thing as 'right' or 'wrong'

Things to remember

▶ When Nietzsche published *The Birth of Tragedy*, it was heavily criticized by scholars for being too ambitious and, to a large extent, naive.

▶ Nietzsche was not the first, or only, person to look back to ancient Greece for more positive values. It was very much within the Romantic tradition.

▶ Nietzsche, from *The Birth of Tragedy* until his last writings, was always critical of the modern man of science and progress, his 'theoretical man'.

▶ Nietzsche is critical of Socrates, and therefore Plato, because of the over-emphasis on the importance of reason and the belief in objective values.

▶ *The Birth of Tragedy* emphasizes the importance of art and, more generally, culture as an affirmation of life. This is in contrast to the scientific, 'deconstructive' picture of the world presented by modern man.

▶ Nietzsche gives us the character of the Greek god Apollo to symbolize especially painting and sculpture.

▶ Nietzsche gives us the character of the Greek god Dionysus to symbolize especially ecstatic music and dance. It is the Dionysian in particular that represents the life force of the universe.

▶ Nietzsche pictures the world as essentially cruel, but vibrant. If, therefore, we are to find any 'truth' at all, we must share in this view of the world.

Fact-check

1 What is *The Birth of Tragedy* about?
   a Persian culture
   b Greek culture
   c German culture
   d Prussian culture

2 What does Nietzsche mean by the 'theoretical man'?
   a The man of science and progress
   b Nietzsche himself
   c Wagner
   d Priests

3 What role did Nietzsche play during the Franco-Prussian War?
   a A drill sergeant
   b A conscientious objector
   c A medical orderly
   d A chef

4 What year did the Franco-Prussian War begin?
   a 1871
   b 1870
   c 1869
   d 1868

5 According to Nietzsche, which Greek playwright killed tragedy?
   a Euripides
   b Sophocles
   c Aeschylus
   d Choerilus

6 Which philosopher did Nietzsche especially criticize for emphasizing reason over the emotions?
   a Hume
   b Locke
   c Socrates
   d Heraclitus

7 Which one of the following books did Nietzsche describe as 'badly written, clumsy, embarrassing...'?

   a Plato's *Republic*

   b Aristotle's *Ethics*

   c Kant's *Critique of Practical Reason*

   d Nietzsche's own work *The Birth of Tragedy*

8 What, for Nietzsche, did Apollo symbolize?

   a Music and dance

   b Painting and sculpture

   c Science and technology

   d Politics and economics

9 What, for Nietzsche, did Dionysus symbolize?

   a Music and dance

   b Painting and sculpture

   c Science and technology

   d Politics and economics

10 What is 'relativism'?

   a The philosophical view that a subjective view of the world is impossible

   b The philosophical view that you should treat your relatives better than your friends

   c The philosophical view that our beliefs are particular to a time and place

   d The philosophical view that nothing exists except what is in the mind

Dig deeper

Douglas Burnham, *Nietzsche's 'The Birth of Tragedy': Reader's Guides* (London: Continuum, 2010)

Paul Raimond Daniels, *Nietzsche and 'The Birth of Tragedy'* (Durham: Acumen, 2013)

5

The revaluation of all values

In this chapter you will learn:

- ▶ *what is meant by 'morality'*
- ▶ *what Nietzsche means when he says, 'God is dead'*
- ▶ *about Nietzsche's naturalism*
- ▶ *about slave morality and* ressentiment.

If we had to label Nietzsche as a particular kind of philosopher, it would be as a moral philosopher. Yet readers are often puzzled by what Nietzsche's moral views actually consist of. This is because – unlike other previous moral philosophers such as Bentham, Mill or Kant – Nietzsche is not prepared to provide the reader with a moral system, method or code. In a sense, it is up to the reader to determine his or her own morality. Nietzsche is therefore primarily concerned with meta-ethical issues and, in fact, is probably the most ruthless critic of the moral philosophical tradition that you will find.

Nietzsche's morality permeates all of his works, but the most systematic works of moral philosophy are *Beyond Good and Evil* and its 'sequel', *On the Genealogy of Morals*.

Nietzsche and moral philosophy

'The overcoming of morality, or even (in a certain sense) the self-overcoming of morality: let that be the name for the long, clandestine work that was kept in reserve for the most subtle and honest (and also the most malicious) people of conscience today, living touchstones of the human heart.'

Beyond Good and Evil, 32

Morality is the branch of philosophy that studies what is good and what is right. It is usually studied from two different perspectives: **normative ethics** and **meta-ethics**. Whereas normative ethics is concerned with what sort of things are good and in providing guidance for moral decision making, meta-ethics (also referred to as analytic ethics) is primarily concerned with what we mean when, for example, we say 'good' or 'bad' or 'just'.

▶ **Normative ethics** may advise us on whether or not an action is morally good or bad – say, to have an abortion – and, in this respect, it can be seen as more concrete and practical.

▶ **Meta-ethics** is more concerned with the language we use – that is, how we define 'good' or 'bad' when we say, for example, 'abortion is good' or 'abortion is bad' – and, in this way, it is of a more abstract nature.

However, just because meta-ethics may be more abstract does not mean that it is any less important: some philosophers would argue that there is little point in looking for guidance as to what is good without understanding what we mean by using the term 'good'. More specifically, meta-ethics attempts to answer such questions as: Where do our morals come from? Are they a product of our culture and history or, when we use the term 'good', for example, are we in some way tapping into a universal goodness that is a law of the universe in perhaps the same way as certain mathematical laws appear to be? If it is the former, then morality is a subjective human invention; if it is the latter, then humans can, theoretically at least, discover objective facts about the universe.

The distinction between normative and meta-ethics is not always a clear one, and certainly many moral philosophers would not have made such a distinction. Whereas meta-ethics has been dominant in twentieth-century moral philosophy, especially in Britain and America, its origins actually rest with the beginning of philosophy proper and the work of Plato (and probably Socrates) some 2,500 years ago. Therefore, there is nothing 'new' about meta-ethics apart from the terminology and a more sophisticated development.

> 'Moral judgement belongs, as does religious judgement, to a
> level of ignorance at which even the concept of the real, the
> distinction between the real and imaginary, is lacking.'
>
> Twilight of the Idols, vii, 1

Spotlight

When *Beyond Good and Evil* was first published, it did not sell well. Nietzsche therefore decided to write 'an expansion and elaboration' of this work, which he called *On the Genealogy of Morals*. He wrote this short work in 1887. In that year there was a major earthquake on the French Riviera, where Nietzsche was residing at the time, which claimed some 2,000 lives. Yet, while people panicked and fled their residences, Nietzsche himself

The death of God

Nietzsche is not so much concerned with the fact that our beliefs are false, but rather with the belief about these beliefs. That is, why should we hold the beliefs that we do? At the beginning of Nietzsche's epitome *Beyond Good and Evil,* he raises the question of why we want truth: why not untruth? It is frequently the career of philosophers to seek for truth, and Nietzsche targets them for his main criticism. He believed the most important question should not be what is true or not but the extent to which a belief supports life and maintains a species. When philosophers make claims to truth, they are merely presenting a preconceived dogma that tells you more about the philosopher's beliefs than anything to do with truths. For Nietzsche, this is especially true in the case of moral philosophy: an attempt to make a science of morals, to establish an objective morality.

'God is dead. God remains dead. And we have killed him.'
The Gay Science, 125

In *The Gay Science*, Nietzsche first declares that God is dead. By this, he means that society no longer has a use for God; the belief does not in any way help the survival of the species; rather, it hinders it. The implications of this are important for ethics, for with the death of God comes the death of religious, especially Christian, morality: a morality that has underpinned Western culture since the fourth century.

Nietzsche's naturalism

Nietzsche is as much a psychologist as he is a philosopher. His interest is in not so much the truth or falsehood of a moral belief, but rather in why human beings prefer one form of morality to another. Nietzsche's philosophy influenced two significant thinkers: the psychoanalyst Sigmund Freud (1856–1939) and the philosopher Michel Foucault (1926–84). Yet, as the Nietzsche scholar Brian Leiter has noted, these two thinkers interpret Nietzsche very differently. On the one hand, Freud saw Nietzsche as a philosopher who revealed deep, hidden facts about human nature that help to explain what we are, while, on the other hand, Foucault praises Nietzsche for denying that there are any facts about human nature! Which of these views is the more accurate understanding of Nietzsche?

The question is an important one in terms of his views on morality because so many moral philosophers before Nietzsche have attempted to establish a moral outlook in the belief that there are facts about human nature. The view that our morality can be based in some way on our nature is referred to as **ethical naturalism**. Famous philosophers who would be considered ethical naturalists include the British utilitarians Jeremy Bentham (1748–1832) and John Stuart Mill (1806–73), and also the German philosopher Immanuel Kant (1724–1804). However, naturalism has its origins with the ancient Greeks, as so much of philosophy does: Aristotle (384–322 BCE) could also be considered a naturalist in his ethics.

As an example of how naturalism works, we can take Bentham's utilitarianism, which works on the principle that it is human nature to avoid pain and pursue pleasure. Given this supposed fact of human nature, Bentham argues that moral decisions should be based on the amount of pain and pleasure the act causes: the greater the amount of happiness, the more morally right the act. Kant, for his part, focused on the rational element of human nature – rather than emotions – and on that basis argued that the best moral decisions are rational decisions. This is an all-too-simplistic account of what are extremely complex ethical theories, but the point is that, if we can determine what is fundamental about our human nature – what makes us tick, so to speak – then we have a sound psychological, semi-scientific basis for our actions.

Spotlight

Jeremy Bentham left his entire estate to University College London after his death. His body is embalmed and sits in a cabinet in the college, although his real head was damaged and so the body now has a wax head. On rare occasions, Bentham is taken out of the cabinet and wheeled into board meetings, where he is recorded as 'present, but not voting'.

The modern view regards Nietzsche also as an ethical naturalist as opposed to Foucault's conception of Nietzsche as denying that there are any facts about nature. It is the 'modern' view because scholarship regarding Nietzsche has changed over the years and certainly in the mid-twentieth century Nietzsche was considered more the champion of existentialism (see Chapter 11): existence precedes essence, we are what we make of ourselves and have no 'function' or 'purpose' aside from what we give ourselves. While it is correct to say that there are existential characteristics of Nietzsche's philosophy, he is perhaps in other respects more of a traditionalist than people might have imagined, despite his 'God is dead' declaration.

We can say with certainty that Nietzsche opposes attempts to find moral truths in some transcendent metaphysics, such as that presented by Plato. Yet it seems curious that Nietzsche is both very critical of the moral philosophical tradition and yet at the same time seems very much a part of it, at least in the naturalist sense. He thinks that every moral system so far produced is naive and, in the case of utilitarianism, 'boneheaded'. Such extreme scepticism and malevolent language understandably suggest that Nietzsche has no time for attempts at moral systems, but the following from *Beyond Good and Evil* gives a different impression:

'For to return man to nature; to master the many conceited and gushing interpretations and secondary meanings that have heretofore been scribbled and painted over that eternal original text homo natura; *to ensure that henceforth man faces man in the same way that currently, grown tough with the discipline of science, he faces the other nature...'*

Beyond Good and Evil, 230

Commentaries often emphasize Nietzsche's reference to the 'discipline of science' in the above quote, and so it has been argued that Nietzsche intends his moral philosophy to be in line with scientific, empirical enquiry. However, while it is one thing to say that metaphysical speculation should be rejected – and this rejection seems a correct reading of Nietzsche – it may be going too far to say that Nietzsche intended his moral philosophy to be based upon scientific discoveries (and by 'scientific' here is meant discoveries in human physiology and psychology especially).

A more accurate reading of the quote above is that Nietzsche wanted moral investigation to be as rigorous as scientific method, not a reflection of scientific discoveries. However, this reading is also somewhat unsatisfactory because, if we are not able to make any reference to scientific facts about nature, it is difficult to see how human beings can be 'translated back into nature'. At best, all Nietzsche seems to be saying here is that we should avoid idle metaphysical speculation, and he often uses terms in his texts such as 'observe better' and 'study more', which suggests that we need to be more disciplined and rigorous in our approach to moral investigation in a way analogous to scientific method.

However, how we are to be 'more disciplined' is not altogether clear, nor is it apparent whether such attempts at scientific rigour would produce positive results. If Nietzsche is simply saying that we should copy scientific methods (in terms of detecting cause and effect) in determining moral actions, then it could well be argued that other suspect disciplines, such as astrology for instance, are justified in their methods. An astrologer looks for causes for actions: the fact that he or she believes those causes to be inherent within the alignment of stars is irrelevant, unless you want to argue that such claims must also be supported by scientific evidence. Therefore, it is not just the method that is important, but the results must also be continuous with the results of science. Only then can we say that astrology is 'bad science'.

However, as shall be shown later in this chapter, Nietzsche makes a number of claims about morality (and other things such as the will to power) that have little or no basis in scientific or empirical evidence. As with his talk of the will to power (see Chapter 6), it seems that we have to see Nietzsche's moral philosophy as an attempt to get us to react, to present a psychological thesis, rather than to argue for any factual account of morality, in which case Nietzsche does not seem to be a naturalist at all, and Foucault may well have been right in his interpretation!

The debate over the degree to which Nietzsche is an ethical naturalist or not is an ongoing one and requires a closer analysis than we have space for here.

Case study: the problem with ethical naturalism: the naturalistic fallacy

Another problem with ethical naturalism more generally, but one that can also be specifically addressed towards Nietzsche if he is a naturalist, is that he could then be accused of what is known as the naturalistic fallacy. The Scottish empiricist philosopher David Hume (1711–76) famously wrote:

'In every system of morality, which I have hitherto met with, I have always remarked, that the author proceeds for some time in the ordinary way of reasoning, and establishes the being of God, or makes observations concerning human affairs; when of a sudden I am surprised to find, that instead of the usual copulations of propositions, is, and is not, I meet with no proposition that is not connected with an ought, or an ought not. This change is imperceptible; but is, however, of the last consequence. For as this ought, or ought not, expresses some new relation or affirmation, 'tis necessary that it should be observed and explained; and at the same time that a reason should be given, for what seems altogether inconceivable, how this new relation can be a deduction from others, which are entirely different from it.'

David Hume, *A Treatise of Human Nature*

What Hume is suggesting here is that moral philosophers are responsible for an error in logic when they move from factual statements to value statements: from an 'is' (fact) to an 'ought' (value). For example, consider the following argument:

1 There are many poor people in the world.
2 The wealthy nations have the financial means to end world poverty.
3 Therefore, the wealthy nations should end world poverty.

Given the first two factual statements above, Hume observes that the conclusion does not logically follow. You could quite easily replace the conclusion with, for example, 'Therefore, the wealthy nations should get wealthier!' While we may be morally outraged by this conclusion, there is nothing logically necessary in the statement that rich nations should help poor nations. For the argument to be logically necessary, it requires deduction – for example:

1 There are many poor people in the world.
2 John is poor.
3 Therefore, John is one of many poor people in the world.

This is a deductive argument because, given factual statements 1 and 2, factual statement 3 follows logically. Importantly here, an 'ought' is not being introduced, just factual statements. The rightness or wrongness of the facts is not an issue here. If you consider utilitarianism again, of which Nietzsche was so critical:

1 Human beings have a given nature.
2 The nature of human beings is to avoid pain and pursue pleasure.
3 Therefore, human beings ought to avoid pain and pursue pleasure.

The first two statements are *factual* (although they could, of course, be wrong), but the third is a *value* statement. Hume brilliantly highlighted a crucial error here, which applies equally to Kant (we *are* rational, therefore we *ought* to be rational) and Aristotle (we *have* a function, therefore we *ought* to fulfil our function). If Nietzsche is also a naturalist, he can be accused of making the same logical error.

Slave morality

Two years after *The Genealogy of Morals*, Nietzsche wrote
Ecce Homo, in which he states the intention of his first essay of
Genealogy:

'The truth of the first essay is the psychology of Christianity:
the birth of Christianity out of the spirit of ressentiment,
not, as is no doubt believed, out of the 'spirit' – essentially a
counter-movement, the great revolt against the domination of
noble *values*'.

Ecce Homo, 'On the Genealogy of Morals: A Polemic'

In fact, Essay 1 is an elaboration of the relatively lengthy
Section 260 of *Beyond Good and Evil*. The very title of the
book, with the use of the word 'genealogy', is important, as it
was provocative at the time to so much as suggest that morals
have a genealogy – that is, a history and development – rather
than adopting the view that morals are just 'there' waiting to
be discovered. This, then, is Nietzsche's main argument in the
whole text but, as stated in Essay 1, morals are not universal
and immutable, but historical products that are therefore
contingent creations of particular people at particular times
with particular motives. The emphasis on motives is important
here, because where Nietzsche is particularly original is in
getting us to question the value of our morals rather than to
assume that moral values are intrinsically valuable.

This enterprise is also indicated in the title *Beyond Good and
Evil*: to understand what we mean when we use moral terms
such as 'good' and 'evil' we need to go beyond them. In addition,
Nietzsche thinks moral philosophers are wrong in believing
that modern man is morally better than past generations and he
especially attacks utilitarianism, the dominant moral theory at
the time.

The fact that Nietzsche claims that our morality has a traceable,
evolved ancestry at all would have shocked many a reader in
his time, for morals were seen as given by the divine lawgiver

God and so there is no genealogy to trace. If the lawgiver disappears, then so does the law and the fear that what will result will be moral anarchy. Yet Nietzsche argues that morality can be explained in naturalistic terms, without the need for a God or gods. They are natural phenomena that have evolved as a result of the need to keep societies together and to check instinctual drives that would destroy the unity of the group if they were allowed free rein. Therefore, morality is a result of circumstance – and it is the circumstance that comes first, which is then followed by morality, not the other way around.

For Nietzsche, therefore, morality:

▶ is a result of circumstance, not the other way round

▶ serves a useful function in that it binds the fabric of the group

▶ can, however, outlive its use and become a hindering custom.

If morality ceases to serve a useful function, yet continues to be maintained by society, this might stunt the growth of that society because we continue to live by rules that are no longer applicable to the world we live in. Nietzsche looked to his own society and saw it to be in a state of decay for this very reason: it looked to the old values, the old Christian values.

When Nietzsche talks of the morality of Western Europe being the product of a particular time and people, what he had in mind in terms of the people were Christian slaves at the time of the Roman Empire, from around the first to the third centuries CE. This is why he refers to the morality of his time as 'slave morality', as opposed to the 'noble morality' possessed by the Romans before the coming of Christianity. What is needed is a new morality. By considering the genealogy of morals, Nietzsche hoped to demonstrate why we have the values we do. This way, if we still continue to hold such values, we are at least aware that they are effectively redundant. Nietzsche's ultimate hope is that we, or perhaps the Superman (see Chapter 7), will create new values.

In considering why Christianity originated with the slaves of the Roman Empire, Nietzsche argued that the slaves saw it as a way of releasing themselves from bondage. As the slaves were not powerful enough to literally free themselves from their masters, they were consoled by religious belief that provided them with spiritual liberation. Christianity, like everything else, is an expression of the will to power. The first Christians were slaves under the Roman Empire and the only way they could assert any kind of superiority over the Romans was to assume a higher spiritual status. This was achieved, according to Nietzsche, by inverting the values of society. For example, the Christians regarded values such as compassion or pity as righteous values that would lead to reward from God, whereas other values such as self-interest were seen as sinful.

Nietzsche argued that the expression of pity is a weapon the weak use against the strong. He criticized the view of pity presented by Schopenhauer and Wagner, who believed that when you feel pity you experience others' suffering as if it were your own, for, at the bottom of Schopenhauer's Will, we are all identical beings. Nietzsche, however, did not believe it was possible to literally feel someone else's pain and, therefore, experience true pity. To want pity is, Nietzsche thought, to want others to suffer with you. Nietzsche observed that the effort of some neurotics to arouse pity in others is because they wish to hurt others and to demonstrate that they at least have this power.

RESSENTIMENT
The real motive for promoting such values was not because there actually is a God that enforces such values, but because the slaves resented the status of the Romans and wanted to possess their power. This is what Nietzsche means by the French term *ressentiment*. The slave feels impotent compared with the master and he is not able to accept the idea that he is treated worse than others. This leads to hostility, to resentment, yet he is unable to release this hostility because of his enslavement. What is the slave to do? He cannot simply use brute force, as this will result in him being in a worse state than before, and so he must use guile.

In order to enact revenge upon his master, the slave uses the weapon of moral conduct. It consists of getting the master to acquiesce to the moral code of the slave and, as a result, appraise himself according to the slave's perspective. As Christians, of course, the slaves do not have the option of revenge, for they should 'turn the other cheek'. However, so successful were the slaves in their guile and secrecy that they managed to disguise their revenge under the cloak of pure intentions.

If the master estimates his own worth according to the values of the slave, he will perceive himself and his actions as evil and reprehensible. His old aristocratic values will be discarded, as he feels morally obliged to do 'good' in the Christian sense. Nietzsche portrays the Roman aristocrat as physically powerful, healthy and aggressive. These qualities remain but, unable to express them externally, they are directed inwards. The aristocrat ends by punishing himself rather than others.

For Nietzsche, slave morality could have arisen only out of hatred and fear. The slave's morality is a reaction to the actions of others. That is, when someone does something to you that you resent, then you class it as 'bad' and, consequently, you create a morality in opposition to this – one that is 'good'. If you are frightened of your neighbour, you react by wanting your neighbour to love you and this is why love is a Christian virtue. The master's morality, however, is not a reaction to others at all. The master has no need to view himself according to the actions of others, but rather affirms himself. He does not require to be loved or for everyone to conform. The master can also hate, but this hatred is discharged in a 'healthy' manner through direct action, rather than, in the case of the weak, through resentment.

Nietzsche is presenting both an historical and psychological portrayal, and it is dubious on both counts. From the psychological point of view, Nietzsche portrays the slave as someone with so much pent-up aggression that it becomes poisonous unless it is expressed in some natural way. This resembles the equally unconvincing psychological theory that children should be allowed to let out their aggression, otherwise it will remain bottled up inside and express itself in later life in some other form. From the historical perspective, we must allow Nietzsche a certain degree of artistic licence, so long as the point is made. He is specifically thinking of Christianity when he talks of religion. Nietzsche was not talking about all religions, for he admired the Greek religion. His main concern with Christianity was its dehumanization: because God is regarded so highly, as perfect and all-good in fact, then it logically follows that man regards himself so lowly, as necessarily imperfect and sinful. Nietzsche did also criticize Jewish slave morality for being the originator of Christian morality.

One of the misunderstandings of Nietzsche's philosophy needs to be made clear at this point. Nietzsche was not an anti-Semite. It is clear from his correspondence that he hated anti-Semites and, in fact, all racist theories. This misunderstanding derives from reading Nietzsche out of context, always a dangerous thing to do, as well as Nietzsche's youthful enthusiasm for Wagner's ideas, and Wagner most definitely was an anti-Semite. Nietzsche's sister Elisabeth, who married an anti-Semite, interpreted her brother's works as anti-Jewish. Nietzsche's language can be easily misinterpreted, especially when he uses such phrases as 'blond beast' (*GM*, 11) when referring to the masters. This has been used as an indication that Nietzsche supported German nationalism and Hitler's views on Aryanism. However, what Nietzsche actually meant by 'blond beast' was a reference to the lion as king of the beasts.

Nonetheless, Nietzsche's views on the master–slave morality are perhaps his most controversial and it is easy to understand why when we consider a few of the main points:

▶ The master morality of the Romans made a distinction between 'good' and 'bad'. 'Good' applies to those who are united, noble and strong. 'Bad' refers to the slaves who are weak and base.

▶ This notion of 'good' and 'bad' therefore is not moral. 'Bad' merely means to be one of the herd, the 'low-minded'. 'Good' means the noble and intellectual.

▶ Christianity reinterpreted 'good' and 'bad' as 'good' and 'evil'. 'Good' was now represented by the life and teaching of Jesus Christ, which included such values as altruism. 'Evil' became what for the masters was previously 'good'.

Nietzsche obviously admires the masters, and there is a certain pro-aristocracy element to him here. Nietzsche evidently approves of a firmly defined class structure and had a disdain for the moral and social mores of the masses. He was certainly very conservative in this respect and was no liberal democrat (see Chapter 10 for his political views).

Criticism of the priests

Nietzsche specifically attacks the Christian (and, before them, the Jewish) priests in their role of promoting the slave morality. The priests were in a unique position in society, in that they were both strong and weak at the same time. They were weak in relation to the aristocratic masters but strong spiritually because they were God's agents on earth. The pastoral, as opposed to the royal, power that the priests possessed was used as a tool for social control and promoting the moral ideal of the herd.

Although he refers to the herd, or slave, morality as promoting the teachings of Christ, Nietzsche places the blame firmly on St Paul as the one who misinterpreted Jesus' teachings. In fact, Nietzsche regards Jesus as a member of the master morality because Jesus was a life affirmer who criticized the Jewish priests for using religion as a means of social control. St Paul, who travelled across the Roman Empire establishing churches in the first century, set the stage for the development of the slave morality and corrupted Jesus' teachings to suit his own ends. The ethic that was endorsed was one of asceticism and self-denial. St Paul was a Roman citizen and was educated in Greek philosophy, and so he made Christianity acceptable to the Romans by incorporating Greek philosophical ideas, especially the Platonic view of dualism. An outlook was presented based on a dualistic world-view: this world being one of necessary suffering but preparation for a better world in the next life. This world was inferior, therefore, to the next world, and the priests had turned Christianity into life denying, instead of Christ's life affirmation.

The idea of the Superman

For Nietzsche, the declaration that 'God is dead' sets humankind free: each person can become his or her own being, the 'Superman'. This morality is a rejection of the herd morality. These are the elite, people who have mastered their own will to power and created life-affirming values to live by. The most crucial value for Nietzsche was that we should be life affirming. The Superman, therefore, is one who realizes the potential of being a human being and is not consoled by a belief in the next life. The Superman has mastered himself and creates his own values.

Nietzsche gave little consideration to the practical implications of his philosophy. He is not a democratic philosopher, for he is not a supporter of the values of the common herd. He believed in the great man, the hero, the Superman, who should be a law unto himself. However, it is difficult to see how a society that consisted of such an elite, one that establishes its own values, would function in society. They would, presumably, look towards the masses with contempt, and one wonders how the Superman could live either among the masses or even among themselves. There would be inevitable conflict, although Nietzsche would have welcomed this, provided it led to a revaluation of values.

Nietzsche's rejection of such Christian values as turning the other cheek, loving your neighbour and compassion for those who are suffering might come across as somewhat callous. For one reason or another, many people are unable to stand on their own two feet or face the realities of life, and so there is a need for compassion. However, Nietzsche did not despise such values as compassion but only the use of them as a psychological prop rather than looking towards one's own resources. Nietzsche's own almost crippling illness plagued him for most of his life, but the last thing he would have wanted was compassion or pity.

However, Nietzsche seems too selective when talking about religion (see Chapter 9 for more on Nietzsche's religious views), asserting the negative while ignoring the variety of religious belief. Even if it were the case that Christianity is the cause of a slave morality, it has also been a vehicle of many revolutionary changes that Nietzsche himself might approve of. The same can be said of many other religions that Nietzsche would regard as 'life denying'. Where does Nietzsche get his values? Nietzsche does not envisage his Superman as someone who is mean, vindictive or indiscriminately violent and cruel. Yet we must wonder why this Superman should not be violent and cruel. How can Nietzsche pick and choose the Superman's morality? Perhaps Nietzsche himself did not fully escape the values of his own religious upbringing.

Key ideas

Normative ethics: the branch of ethics concerned with deciding what sort of things are good and providing practical guidance for moral decision making

Meta-ethics (also referred to as analytic ethics): the branch of ethics primarily concerned with what we mean when, for example, we say 'good' or 'bad' or 'just'

Utilitarianism: a moral theory that works on the principle that it is human nature to avoid pain and pursue pleasure: the greater the amount of happiness, the more morally right the act

Ethical naturalism: the view that our morality can be based in some way on our nature

Ressentiment (the French word for 'resentment'): term used in Nietzsche's genealogy of morals – the hostility that the slave feels towards the master

Things to remember

▶ Nietzsche is primarily concerned with meta-ethical issues rather than normative ethics.

▶ Nietzsche is highly critical of just about every moral system that has been presented in the history of philosophy so far.

▶ Nietzsche made his famous remark 'God is dead. God remains dead. And we have killed him' in his book *The Gay Science*.

▶ Nietzsche's morality is notoriously difficult to interpret, although we can say with certainty that he was opposed to the belief in objective moral truths.

▶ In Essay 1 of *On The Genealogy of Morals*, Nietzsche describes how modern 'herd morality' derives historically from the early Christians.

▶ By the French term *ressentiment*, Nietzsche means the expression of a feeling of inferiority and powerlessness.

▶ The Supermen are those who declare that 'God is dead' and, consequently, create their own morality.

▶ Nietzsche was not so much concerned with providing a table of values. What mattered was that values should be life-affirming.

Fact-check

1 What is normative ethics concerned with?
  a What it means to be morally normal
  b What we mean when we use terms such as 'good' or 'bad'
  c Concrete, practical guidance
  d An ethical theory that argues for the greatest happiness for the greatest number

2 What is meta-ethics concerned with?
  a Ethics that come from metaphysics
  b How moral language is used and what we mean by it.
  c Concrete, practical guidance
  d An ethical theory that argues for the greatest happiness for the greatest number

3 What is ethical naturalism?
  a The view that we can determine what is right and wrong from our nature
  b The view that we would all be better people morally if we shed our clothing
  c An ethical theory that argues for the greatest happiness for the greatest number
  d The view that nature is cruel

4 What is utilitarianism?
  a An ethical theory that argues for the greatest happiness for the greatest number
  b An ethical theory that argues that we get our morals from reason
  c An ethical theory that our morality comes from God
  d The view that it is not possible to establish an ethical theory

5 Which one of the following philosophers was a utilitarian?
  a Immanuel Kant
  b John Stuart Mill
  c Friedrich Nietzsche
  d Arthur Schopenhauer

6 What is the naturalistic fallacy?

    a An error in logic when you move from factual statements to value statements

    b The incorrect belief that anything is natural

    c The incorrect belief that nature can tell us anything

    d The view that you can derive an 'ought' from an 'is'

7 What is *ressentiment*?

    a Nietzsche's favourite French dessert

    b The hostility that the master feels towards the slave

    c The subtitle of Nietzsche's work *Beyond Good and Evil*

    d The hostility that the slave feels towards the master

8 What is 'slave morality'?

    a A particular reference to the morality of the Christian slaves during the time of the Roman Empire

    b The view that slavery is moral

    c The view that slavery is immoral

    d Nietzsche's view that the working classes were enslaved and should rebel against the elite

9 How does slave morality emerge?

    a From love and compassion

    b From hatred and fear

    c From hunger and poverty

    d From power and wealth

10 Who does Nietzsche blame for the herd morality?

    a Jesus

    b St Paul

    c The Pope

    d The Superman

Dig deeper

Daniel Conway, *Nietzsche's* On the Genealogy of Morals: *A Reader's Guide* (London: Continuum International Publishing Group, 2008)

Lawrence J. Hatab, *Nietzsche's 'On the Genealogy of Morality': An Introduction* (Cambridge: Cambridge University Press, 2008)

Brian Leiter, *The Routledge Philosophy Guidebook to Nietzsche on Morality* (London: Routledge, 2002)

6

The will to power

In this chapter you will learn:

▶ *how important the will to power is for Nietzsche's philosophy*

▶ *to what extent the will to power can be seen as an explanation for how the world works*

▶ *to what extent the will to power can be seen as a subjective phenomenon*

▶ *a possible third explanation of the will to power as providing an empirical account of the world.*

Typically, Nietzsche does not do us the favour of giving us a nice, friendly, accessible account of his 'doctrine' of the will to power. In fact, it is hardly a 'doctrine' at all, hence the inverted commas. The debate over what the will to power actually is and how much importance should be attached to it centres on two different interpretations:

▶ An objective explanation for everything: Nietzsche wants to give us a metaphysical picture of the world – a 'theory of everything' that explains the world of experience but that is, nonetheless, 'beyond' the physical (hence 'metaphysical')

▶ A subjective interpretation: this is not asserting that there is a world 'out there' beyond the physical, but is simply explaining the will to power as subjective.

Both these interpretations will be considered, as well as a possible third interpretation, but first it will help to speculate on why there exist such diverse understandings and how much importance should be attributed to this doctrine.

The enigma of the will to power

'What is good? – All that heightens the feeling of power, the will to power, power itself in man. What is bad? – All that proceeds from weakness. What is happiness? – The feeling that power increases – that a resistance is overcome...'

The Anti-Christ, 2

The will to power is certainly one of the most famous contributions that Nietzsche made to philosophy, yet it is also a concept subject to a variety of differing interpretations by scholars. As said already, Nietzsche, for his part, is not always helpful in his own articulation of the will to power either, which inevitably opens him up to speculation and disagreement among his readers. Much writing on the will to power, especially early scholarship, places this concept at the heart of Nietzsche's philosophy, as the underlying concept for all of his philosophical views on such things as morality, art and nature. More recent scholarship, however, has raised questions about whether Nietzsche really gives us a strong doctrine of the will to power at all.

Has the importance of the will to power for Nietzsche's philosophy been overplayed? It is certainly curious that Nietzsche seemed to drop any reference to the will to power in his last major work, *Ecce Homo*. This omission is significant because in this work Nietzsche reflects upon his ideas in all his previous works. To make no mention of the will to power at all certainly suggests that he no longer considered it important. In addition, in 1886 Nietzsche wrote a series of new prefaces to *The Birth of Tragedy, Human, All Too Human, Dawn* and *The Gay Science* in which he reflected upon his major philosophical themes, yet the will to power was again not mentioned.

Spotlight

The 'Dig deeper' section at the end of this chapter cites the work on Nietzsche by the philosopher Martin Heidegger. It is an interesting read but should be treated with caution, for Heidegger saw the will to power as Nietzsche's real philosophy and his unpublished works as truly reflecting what Nietzsche meant, rather than what he chose to publish. In fact, Heidegger stated that the Superman is embodied in the Nazi SS tank commander!

However, although he may have decided against developing the will to power as a doctrine in his published works, this is not to say that the doctrine had ceased to preoccupy him – quite the opposite, in fact. The reason Nietzsche wrote new prefaces for many of his earlier books was because he was in the process of changing publishers after learning that his old publisher had two-thirds of his books stuffed in a warehouse with little attempt to push sales. After writing books for 15 years, it would have been a huge disappointment to Nietzsche to discover that his publisher had made little effort to sell his books. By launching with a new publisher, Nietzsche hoped for a fresh beginning, and so he wrote a series of new prefaces. He also decided to start a new work with the title *The Will to Power: Attempt at a New Interpretation of Everything That Happens*. The title alone is quite revealing and does suggest that Nietzsche believed in at least the possibility of the will to power as an important contribution to his philosophical enterprise. This project became almost an obsession (and certainly a therapeutic aid against depression) for Nietzsche and, for that reason, if for no other, it should not be surprising that his sister and Peter Gast should collect his notes together into a work with the title *The Will to Power*.

Nietzsche's project was intended to be a major four-volume work with a coherent structure, unlike his previous collections of aphorisms and short essays. In the autumn of 1888 he completed what he meant to be the first volume, *The Anti-Christ*, but it ended up being the whole work itself. Nietzsche had previously given up on the title *The Will to Power* anyway, and was leaning towards 'Revaluation of All Values', which, in retrospect, seems more fitting to his lifelong enterprise. He wrote, 'My revaluation of all values, which has *The Anti-Christ* as its main title, is finished.'

It is perhaps going too far to say that Nietzsche placed no importance on the will to power. The terms 'will to power' and 'power' are used explicitly throughout many of his works, as well as implicitly. The fact that Nietzsche was so preoccupied with it through much of his sane life also suggests that it has some value, even if he saw it more as a tentative experiment than a fully worked-out doctrine.

'And do you know what "the world" is to me? Shall I show it to you in my mirror? This world: a monster of energy, without beginning, without end; a firm, iron magnitude of force that does not grow bigger or smaller, that does not expend itself but only transforms itself; as a whole of unalterable size, a household without expenses or losses, but likewise without increase or income; enclosed by "nothingness" as by a boundary; not something blurry or wasted, not something endlessly extended, but set in a definite space as a definite force, and not a space that might be "empty" here or there, but rather as a force throughout, as a play of forces and waves of forces [...] do you want a name for this world? A solution for all its riddles? A light

> 'Assuming, finally, that we could explain our entire instinctual
> life as the development and differentiation of one basic form
> of the will (namely the will to power, as my tenet would have
> it); assuming that one could derive all organic functions from
> this will to power and also find in it the solution of the problem
> of procreation and alimentation (it is all one problem), then
> we would have won the right to designate all effective energy
> unequivocally as: the will to power. The world as it is seen from
> the inside, the world defined and described by its "intelligible
> character" – would be simply "will to power" and that alone.'
>
> Beyond Good and Evil, 36

The objective interpretation

The traditional view looks to the will to power as an
explanation for all of life's manifestations. It is a neutral 'force'
governing the world that is akin to Schopenhauer's concept of
the Will, considered in Chapter 2. The best way to understand
this view of the will to power is to look at the quote above from
the collected notes *The Will to Power*.

This passage has its attractions in its picture of the world as a
'monster of energy' and seems to point to a belief on Nietzsche's
part in some underlying principle, a 'theory of everything'.
To support this interpretation, some scholars would cite the
importance of the Presocratics for Nietzsche who, on the whole,
were distinguished by the belief that there is an underlying
principle that governs the universe, an *arche* (first principle)
that is the origin of and responsible for all things. For example,
the Greek philosopher Thales (*c.*625–545 BCE) presented a
form of **material monism**: that the universe consists ultimately

of only one substance. What makes Thales stand out here was his pronouncement that there are fundamental features of the universe that are not immediately accessible to the senses or to 'common sense'. It makes us think that the world is not as it at first seems: there are inner workings to be uncovered. Thales was not so concerned with the Homeric gods at play, but adopted a materialist view that all things were made of material substance and that it is possible to uncover patterns and laws for this material stuff. Thales, in his case, concluded that the seeming multiplicity of the universe can be reduced to the fundamental substance of water – which, of course, is wrong, but at least he began the philosophical enterprise of seeking an underlying explanation for all things.

Case study: Thales

In looking at the history of philosophy in the Western world, Thales is a good starting point. He was a 'Presocratic', which simply means 'one who comes before Socrates' (although, in fact, a number of the 'Presocratics' were contemporary with Socrates). The Presocratics are important in understanding what philosophy is all about and how it can be distinguished from other disciplines. It is also important to understand that Plato did not emerge from a cultural vacuum; the kind of philosophical questions he was asking (What is knowledge? What is the best life? What is right and wrong?) were the same questions that philosophers before him were engaged with.

Thales was born in the town of Miletus on the Anatolian coast, just south of the island of Samos – the first 'Greek' philosopher was actually from what is now Turkey. However, during the time of Thales, Miletus was a Greek (or, rather, Hellenic) city-state, a modern city that was wealthy and, due to its involvement in commerce with other nations, aware of differing beliefs. Certainly, the fact that the city's wealth and cosmopolitan nature allowed some people at least to engage in such leisurely activities as thinking and to have access to knowledge of other ideas goes some way in explaining why philosophy began when and where it did. But, also, in many respects the Presocratics were quite 'modern' in that their philosophical investigations were very 'scientific'. The need for trade and commerce was a motivating force in trying to understand nature, astronomy and the art of navigation, and there is a story that Thales was so preoccupied with looking up at the stars that he once fell into a pothole as a result.

Thales' conclusion that the world consists of water is wrong, of course, but the important point here is that he does get us to question whether the world is really as it seems: that there are fundamental features of the universe that are not immediately accessible to the senses or to 'common sense'. Where the Greek myth-makers such as Homer and Hesiod looked for explanations with the gods, Thales looked for more natural explanations.

Is this, then, what Nietzsche's doctrine of the will to power is? Is it the view that the underlying principles of the universe are a multiplicity of drives seeking power over one another? This may be one possible understanding, to be explored further in this chapter, but we need to be aware that things are not that simple. Taken at face value, the much-quoted passage above certainly seems to assert that the will to power is an all-encompassing phenomenon – the very essence of life itself: 'This world is the will to power – and nothing besides!' But we need to be very careful of our sources when reading Nietzsche. The above quote from section 1067 of *The Will to Power* is from a work that has been much discredited, as it is really a compilation of Nietzsche's notes edited by his sister who had her own political and ideological agenda. In fact, Nietzsche himself had discarded the passage in 1887, and so he would not have endorsed its publication, thus giving it a printed status it does not deserve.

We must look to works that Nietzsche wished to be published to see whether a 'theory of everything' thesis can be supported. Interestingly, Nietzsche, throughout the whole of his works, presents only one argument (if 'argument' is the right word here) for the will to power. This is contained in Section 36 of *Beyond Good and Evil*, which is the second quote in the section above.

Does this really differ that much from the quote from *The Will to Power*? In very subtle ways it does, but the subtlety – in Nietzsche's case – is always important. Nietzsche was a trained philologist, remember, and he chose his words carefully. If you read *The Will to Power* passage again, you will note how assertive it is, how certain; but these were notes not intended to be published. When it actually comes to writing something for intended publication, Nietzsche is more circumspect in his choice of words, more cautious. For example, he starts off with the word 'Assuming' and then uses words such as 'if' followed by 'then'. The important point that Nietzsche is trying to get across is that we should not remain silent or be sceptical on such topics, but that we should realize that when we attempt to contemplate metaphysical 'truths' we are confronted with the problem of how to actually understand 'truth'. This is the type of puzzle, conundrum or riddle that Nietzsche is very fond of.

When scholars interpret Nietzsche they sometimes forget the importance he places on the use of language, as well as his own playfulness with words and his expertise in the ancient Greek tradition of irony. By using such terms as 'intelligible character' – put into inverted commas by Nietzsche – he is making a reference to Kant and his belief in the world 'in itself', but Nietzsche himself does not assert that there is a world 'in itself', a noumenal world separate from the world of appearance. Rather, supposing it would be possible for there to be a world 'in itself', it would actually be no different from the world of appearance.

Whereas Nietzsche's earlier writings may suggest a view of the will to power as akin to Schopenhauer's will to life, as an explanation for all phenomena, the essence to life itself, by the time of his more mature work – and in particular in his 'trilogy' of *Thus Spoke Zarathustra, Beyond Good and Evil* and *The Genealogy of Morals*, Nietzsche had seemingly rejected this view. Consider this passage from *Thus Spoke Zarathustra*:

'He who shot the doctrine of "will to existence" at truth certainly did not hit the truth: this will – does not exist! Only where life is, there is also will: not will to life, but – so I teach you – will to power! The living creature values many things higher than life itself; yet out of this evaluation itself speaks – the will to power! Thus life once taught me: and with this teaching do I solve the riddle of your hearts, you wisest men.'

Thus Spoke Zarathustra, II. 12

Here, Nietzsche is rejecting Schopenhauer's metaphysical doctrine of the Will, and so it would be surprising if the replacement of this with the will to power is also meant to be metaphysical, in which case how would it differ at all from Schopenhauer? Also, in his mature work, Nietzsche is explicit – as much as he ever is explicit – in his rejection of metaphysical speculation. For example, in his preface to *Beyond Good and Evil* he considers such 'philosophical dogmatism' to be 'some folk superstition from time immemorial… some play on words perhaps, some seductive aspect of grammar, or a daring generalization from very limited, very personal, very human, all-too-human facts', and then, in Section 1, he considers a belief in metaphysical truths as the 'prejudice' of philosophers. Or consider the title of one section of *The Twilight of the Idols*: 'How the Real World Finally Became a Fable'. With such explicit attacks on metaphysics, it is certainly difficult to sustain a view that Nietzsche's will to power is metaphysical in character.

Those scholars who have attempted to argue that Nietzsche's will to power is a reference to the underlying 'substance' of the world, to the world as a 'monster of energy, without beginning, without end' (*WP*, 1067) have had to rely mostly upon the discredited work *The Will to Power* as their source. Attractive though this concept of the will to power may be, it does not stand up to scrutiny when seen in the light of works that Nietzsche intended to have published. In fact, to suggest that Nietzsche wanted to put forward a 'theory of everything' may well go against what he stood for. For example, when we read what Nietzsche said in *Beyond Good and Evil*:

'… what formerly happened with the Stoics still happens today, too, as soon as any philosophy begins to believe in itself. It always creates the world in its own image.'

Beyond Good and Evil, 9

This passage can be read in a number of ways: on the one hand, he is accusing the Stoics of imposing a particular view upon nature; on the other, Nietzsche seems to be suggesting this is something that philosophy inevitably does. While he may be criticizing the Stoics for 'creating the world in its own image', he seems to be admitting that this is unavoidable. Is Nietzsche acknowledging that his speculations on the will to power are an assertion of some underlying fact about nature while also being aware that any assertions, any statements of 'facts', are ultimately the philosopher's own prejudices? Such ambiguities are typical of Nietzsche and there is certainly a tension between Nietzsche speaking of nature in terms of universal, natural laws, and his constant warning against engaging in such metaphysical speculation.

The subjective interpretation

> '... somebody with an opposite intention and mode of interpretation could come along and be able to read from nature, and with reference to the same set of appearances, a tyrannically ruthless and pitiless execution of power claims. This sort of interpreter would show the unequivocal and unconditional nature of all "will to power" so vividly and graphically that almost every word, and even the word "tyranny", would ultimately seem useless [...] Granted, this is only an interpretation too – and you will be eager enough to make this objection? – well then, so much the better.'
>
> Beyond Good and Evil, 22

The final sentence of the quote above is particularly instructive as it appears to be an admission that his talk of the will to power is his own interpretation and is therefore no 'truer' than that put forward by any other philosopher. But if it is indeed the case that the will to power is no more true than any other view of the world, and if Nietzsche knows he is putting forward his own subjective view, then why give it any credence?

To answer this, it is important to remember how much value needs to be placed on Nietzsche's style: on his use of metaphor, ambiguity, riddles, humour and irony. Nietzsche knows he is seeing the world from his own perspective, for how can he – or anybody else for that matter – do otherwise? Nonetheless, the knowledge that one cannot demonstrate objective truths, that one cannot step outside one's own perspective, is not a reason to remain silent or to adopt a nihilistic stance towards our values. Nietzsche, remember, is very positive; he does not bury his head in despair and existential nausea (although he has his moments), but rejoices in the realization that we cannot know what is true. Nietzsche, however, does not stop using words such as 'truth' and 'soul', but these words for Nietzsche mean something different. He writes about the will to power because he values it, not because it necessarily exists 'out there'.

Such a reading of Nietzsche is inevitably problematic as we are then faced with the dilemma of when, if ever, he is not talking metaphorically. Are we to say that all of his philosophy – his views on slave morality, on the Superman, on tragedy and so forth – is his own prejudice; that there are no genuine truth-claims in any of his writings at all? Even if we accept that this is the case, it does not necessarily follow that we should reject Nietzsche's writings, any more than we should reject anyone else's writings on the basis that they are value-preferences.

The importance of a doctrine, of a teaching, lies here with the reader: Nietzsche often said that he was addressing a small audience, a 'select few' (although he was not so lacking in vanity as to not wish that more people would buy his books), and so, provided they found something appealing in his writings, he has succeeded. Novels, the best novels anyway, tend to reveal something about the world or/and about human nature, and the same can be said about many religious texts, whether you believe in the truth-claims of religion or not. The Bible, for example, can be read on many levels; at one level the reader may read it from an 'anti-realist' stance, that is, rejecting the theological claims that there is a God or that Jesus is the son of God, while still reading the book as revealing 'truths' about human beings, their motives, drives and so on. It is therefore perhaps not that surprising that Nietzsche often writes in a poetical, literary and – certainly in *Thus Spoke Zarathustra* – biblical manner, frequently resorting to parables. 'Truths' are revealed at the psychological level. That is to say, the will to power tells us a lot about how human beings – and possibly other organic species – interact with one another, what motivates them, and it may well help to explain the origin of our beliefs and values. In that sense, Nietzsche's writings are a valuable contribution to knowledge.

If we see Nietzsche's views as a subjective interpretation that some of his readers can relate to, what does this reveal about the nature of the will to power? It will help if it can be determined what Nietzsche is *not* saying: we are not, for example, striving for power all the time. That would imply that even when we are sleeping we are striving for power, or that every activity – however seemingly pointless – is an expression of the will to power. In addition, we are not always motivated by power. For example, watching a programme on TV or sightseeing in Paris does not seem to have any power-motivation behind it, although, in given circumstances, presumably it can. The will to power, rather, is one drive among many, albeit an important one.

Given the importance of language and communication for Nietzsche, it seems appropriate to look to *Thus Spoke Zarathustra* as it is here that we can find Nietzsche's more systematic elaboration of the will to power as interpretation. In the second part of *Thus Spoke Zarathustra* – the chapter entitled 'Of Self-overcoming' – Zarathustra declares: 'Where I found a living creature, there I found will to power.' The importance of the title of this chapter in his elaboration of the will to power should not be overlooked: of self-overcoming, or self-transcendence. Rather than the will to power being conceived as some underlying principle of the world, it is seen first and foremost as the power over one's self.

Reading the story of Zarathustra, we have a character in the process of creation: creation of a new kind of world with new values. In this sense, Zarathustra can be seen as mirroring Nietzsche's own philosophical enterprise. When faced with a world that no longer had meaning or credibility in his eyes (and, Nietzsche believed, in the eyes of a select, although growing, number of others), he creates a world that does have meaning for him. Again, the issue of whether it is 'true' or not is something of an irrelevance or, at best, merely highlighting the whole problem of trying to look at the world in polar opposites of 'true' or 'false'. Nietzsche often saw his Supermen as creative artists, painters and musicians and so the importance of creating a world for oneself that has value is a philosophical and artistic enterprise.

Related to this self-overcoming is self-enhancement. While we can possibly survive in a world that lacks meaning, Nietzsche questions whether such a life is worth living. Self-preservation is one thing, but self-enhancement – the bettering of one's self – is another. In fact, mere self-preservation will inevitably lead to decay and destruction, whereas enhancement ensures that we survive, and survive as better human beings. The will to power is when we say 'yes' to life and go on the offensive against mediocrity and what Nietzsche saw as decadent values.

Nietzsche's first exploration into the will to power has its origins in *The Birth of Tragedy,* when he talks of the interaction of the Dionysian and Apollonian artistic life forces (see Chapter 4). An expression of the will to power is to make sense of the world, to give it meaning. By making sense of the world, humankind overpowers it and brings it into a form that is in accordance with the self. The world reflects the self and the self recognizes its role within the world. Nietzsche saw this as a dangerous enterprise – life threatening and sanity threatening – because most people, Nietzsche believed, prefer to live life 'herd-like' and unthinking, rather than confront their place in the world.

What is understood by 'truth', then, is whatever overcomes the world, whatever view of the world prevails. Truth is a mental construct; it is what is psychologically bearable. Early on in *Thus Spoke Zarathustra*, the prophet – rather naively, it turns out – says the following: 'To lure many away from the herd – that is why I have come. The people and the herd shall be angry with me: the herdsmen shall call Zarathustra a robber' (*TSZ*, I.9).

In many ways, the mission of Zarathustra – and that of Nietzsche, too – is like that of Socrates as Plato pictured him in his famous analogy of the cave. Briefly, in this analogy, prisoners are tied together at the bottom of the cave and spend their lives staring at shadows on the wall. The prisoners take these shadows to be reality. One day a prisoner is released and exits the cave. The released prisoner is then 'enlightened' to what the world is really like and feels duty bound to return to the bottom of the cave and free his fellow prisoners. Plato uses this analogy to illustrate the role of the philosopher, and the freed prisoner can be seen as embodied in the character of Socrates who saw it as his duty to go among the people of Athens and to question their deeply set values. Zarathustra saw his role in a similar manner, but the key difference between Socrates and Zarathustra (or, more accurately, between Plato and Nietzsche) is that the former saw 'truth' in a metaphysical way, whereas the latter saw 'truth' as a subjective, psychological phenomenon: a turning into one's self rather than gazing at the stars above.

The empirical interpretation

So far two possible interpretations of the will to power have been presented:

▶ the objective interpretation of the world: a metaphysical picture

▶ the subjective interpretation of the world with psychological implications.

A third interpretation is that, although Nietzsche did not intend to propose the will to power as metaphysical, he nonetheless wanted to say that it is much more than merely subjective. That is, he wanted to present it as an empirical, scientific explanation of the physical world without any reference to a metaphysical world: that is, that our experience tells us that the world can be explained by the will to power. Through our senses and our observations of nature and how it operates, is it possible to explain its goings-on as will to power and nothing else? This seems much more scientific than speculative, in the same way that some scientists today look for a 'theory of everything'. Also, Nietzsche was not so anti-science, and could be quite positive about the role of science generally.

This view that the world, or at least the organic (which does, of course, also include the human) world, is will to power has been labelled the 'cosmological' doctrine of the will to power by the scholar Maudemarie Clark, although Clark goes on to say that Nietzsche does not actually present us with a cosmological doctrine at all. However, some would argue, the passage from Section 36 of *Beyond Good and Evil* quoted above does seem to suggest at least a biological conception of the will to power. In another part of Section 36, Nietzsche says, 'all mechanical events, in so far as energy is active in them, are really the energy of the will, the effect of the will', and in the previous paragraph in the same section he talks about 'organic processes' in a similar manner. Given this, is Clark right to deny the cosmological view?

We need to consider what kind of picture the 'cosmos' would be if we were to say it is the 'will to power'? One analogy that has been used is that, just as the state is made up of a collection of individuals, the world is made up of a collection of 'wills'. This form of analogy was not an uncommon one in Nietzsche's day: while sociologists saw society as an organism, biologists compared the organism to how society functions; and Nietzsche certainly liked reading the contemporary theories of biologists, zoologists, embryologists, physiologists and the like. It is nonetheless difficult to picture Nietzsche's world, despite the use of analogy. One scientist with whom Nietzsche was familiar is Charles Darwin, and there is a possibility that Nietzsche's world is Darwinian: the will to power as a product of natural selection whereby the world is made up of components fighting for dominance over one another. However, it is still unclear what these 'components' are. What, in other words, does Nietzsche mean by the will? Is the biological world made up of lots of 'little wills' striving for dominance and, if this is the case, do these wills have any sense of self-awareness?

Spotlight

Nietzsche certainly had an enthusiasm for science, but it must be kept in mind that, at that time, all philosophy was considered to be 'science' in some respects. Today we make a distinction between what we regard as the 'natural sciences' (such as physics and chemistry) and the 'spiritual-intellectual sciences', which we may now call philosophy. While Nietzsche certainly found pleasure in his reading of the natural sciences, he was nonetheless critical of the belief that scientists are able to discover what the world is really, objectively like. No doubt, if Nietzsche were alive today, he would have little patience for Richard Dawkins.

The suggestion that the will involves someone or something willing does not seem to fit with Nietzsche's views on the self – the ego. For example, the French philosopher René Descartes (1596–1650) argued famously for a self in his expression: 'I think, therefore I am.' In other words, for there to be thoughts there must be a thinker. Similarly, for there to be will, there must be a subject doing the willing. In this sense, 'will' can be equated with 'desire'. But Nietzsche clearly rejects the idea that there is a self at all; he does not accept the seemingly logical consequence that a thought requires a thinker and therefore his talk of 'will' does not need to be seen in terms of subjects desiring something. 'Will' is not a conscious thing but something much more abstract. Perhaps 'will' is better described as 'drives', one of which is the drive for power. Other drives may, for example, include the sex drive, the survival drive and the pleasure drive.

The drive for power over others can in one way be seen as a separate drive, but also it could be seen as that which is common to all drives, for all kinds of drives 'want' to dominate other drives. The world, then, is seen as a collection of organisms with distinctive drives that compete against one another for dominance. The human being, likewise, is seen as composed of a collection of competing drives.

The picture of the world as a bundle of organisms striving for power over one another may have its advocates, but it nonetheless remains open to speculation and a series of unanswered questions. If nothing else, it seems a rather simplistic and naive picture that is neither philosophical nor particularly empirical. Are there really any grounds to suggest that every action in the world, every event, every cause and effect, has as its impetus in the will to power in the sense Nietzsche seems to suggest? Fortunately, various passages in Nietzsche's works suggest that he did not consider that the world was 'will to power and nothing besides'. For example, take the following passage:

> 'Life itself is to my mind the instinct for growth, for durability, for an accumulation of forces, for power: where the will to power is lacking there is decline. It is my contention that all the supreme values of mankind lack this will.'
>
> The Anti-Christ, 6

The passage is enlightening because, on the one hand, Nietzsche says that life itself is the instinct for power, but he also states that the will to power can be 'lacking'. If something is lacking the will to power, then it does not make sense to say that everything is the will to power. In the same way, one molecule of water is two hydrogen atoms covalently bonded to a single oxygen atom. If you then say that one molecule is lacking an oxygen atom, then it makes little sense to still call it 'water'. Indeed, there are a number of other references in Nietzsche's works that suggest that the will to power is not the one underlying substance of the world, but rather one characteristic of the universe among others (such as desires, effects and so on).

Conclusion

Is the subjective understanding of the will to power the most accurate account of this enigma? While a metaphysical understanding of the will to power seems way off the mark, given what Nietzsche has to say about metaphysics and those philosophers who subscribe to a world 'out there', we also need to be cautious in arguing that Nietzsche was entirely proposing a subjective, psychological account. His eagerness to devour the writings of his contemporary theorizers in the realms of biology, physiology, embryology and the like, points to a certain degree of empathy for their views. Nietzsche at times can come across as strongly empirical and it would not be too far-fetched to suggest that, although he emphasized the subjective account of the will to power above all else, he ambitiously hoped – perhaps vainly – to underpin it in an empirical account of how the world actually seemed to operate.

Key ideas

Will to power: a concept elaborated in the works of Nietzsche where, at the most basic level, he regards it as an important driving 'force'; however, what he means by that is subject to different interpretations

Material monism: the view that the universe consists of only one substance

Arche: the Greek word for an underlying principle that governs the universe

Things to remember

▶ Opinion is divided over how important the will to power is for Nietzsche, and even over what it means exactly. Nonetheless, Nietzsche spent a lot of time on the concept, especially in his notes.

▶ When we read what Nietzsche has to say about the will to power in his notes, we need to treat these views with caution, as they were never intended for publication.

▶ One interpretation of the will to power is that it is an attempt to explain everything in a metaphysical sense, but this is unlikely given Nietzsche's views on metaphysics.

▶ Another, more likely, interpretation of the will to power is that it is a subjective interpretation. By 'subjective', Nietzsche means that there are no objective truths, and so he cannot make claim to the will to power as objectively true. However, the 'truth' of the will to power can nonetheless be achieved at the psychological level in that it tells us something about ourselves and the world we live in.

▶ A third possible interpretation of the will to power is that it is based on available, empirically observable data.

Fact-check

1 Which one of the following is *not* a Nietzsche doctrine?
   a The will to power
   b The Superman
   c Existence precedes essence
   d *Ressentiment*

2 Which one of the following is a definition of material monism?
   a The desire for material things
   b That the universe consists of only one substance
   c That the universe consists of many substances
   d That the universe is driven by capitalism

3 Which one of the following works by Nietzsche is a collection of his unpublished notes?
   a *Ecce Homo*
   b *The Anti-Christ*
   c *The Will to Power*
   d *Beyond Good and Evil*

4 What is the name of Plato's analogy in which a prisoner is freed and becomes 'enlightened'?
   a The cave analogy
   b The ship analogy
   c The tunnel analogy
   d The mountain analogy

5 Which Greek philosopher can be compared to Zarathustra's mission to go among the people and question their values?
   a Thales
   b Socrates
   c Aristotle
   d Apollo

6 Which one of the following is a definition of metaphysics?
   a The unifying force of the universe
   b Speculation on what exists beyond the physical world
   c The study of physics by really intelligent people
   d The belief that God exists

7 Which philosopher said, 'I think, therefore I am'?

  a Immanuel Kant

  b Friedrich Nietzsche

  c René Descartes

  d Socrates

8 Which philosopher believed that the universe consists of one underlying substance of water?

  a Socrates

  b Aristotle

  c Kant

  d Thales

9 What does it mean to see the world as 'Darwinian'?

  a A world made up of components fighting for dominance over one another – that is, governed by natural selection

  b A world in which all creatures live at peace with one another

  c A world in which all life derives from Noah's Ark

  d A world in which all life has been created by a deity

10 Which one of the following is *not* a possible interpretation of the will to power?

  a The will to power as presenting an objective, metaphysical picture of the world

  b The will to power as a subjective interpretation of the world that has psychological implications

  c An empirical, scientific explanation of the physical world

  d The view that the world should be ruled by Supermen who enslave those with less power

Dig deeper

Martin Heidegger, *Nietzsche*, trans. David Farell Krell (New York: HarperCollins, 1991)

Rudiger Safranski, *Nietzsche: A Philosophical Biography* (London: Granta, 2003)

Rex Welshon, *The Philosophy of Nietzsche* (Montreal: McGill-Queen's University Press, 2004)

7

Zarathustra, the Superman and the eternal recurrence

In this chapter you will learn:

▶ *about the story of* Thus Spoke Zarathustra
▶ *what Nietzsche meant by the 'Superman'* (Übermensch)
▶ *about the eternal recurrence*
▶ *about Nietzsche's views on nihilism*
▶ *about* amor fati.

Although not considered his best philosophical work, *Thus Spoke Zarathustra* is Nietzsche's most widely read book. In many respects, the foundations for that book can be found in *Human, All Too Human* and *Dawn*, especially in the introduction of the concept of the will to power (see Chapter 6). The importance of *Thus Spoke Zarathustra* rests not only on its literary style but also on the fact that it contains the fullest exposition so far of his theories on the will to power, the Superman and the eternal recurrence.

Thus Spoke Zarathustra

> 'My formula for greatness in a human being is amor fati: that one wants nothing to be other than it is, not in the future, not in the past, not in all eternity.'
>
> *Ecce Homo*, 'Why I Am So Clever', 10

The original Zarathustra invented the concept of good and evil as an eternal war of battling opposites. However, Nietzsche's Zarathustra aimed to show that we must go beyond the concepts of good and evil. For Nietzsche, the historical Zarathustra represents what can be achieved through the will to power, and his belief that every person is responsible for his or her own destiny would have struck a chord with Nietzsche.

Thus Spoke Zarathustra is in four parts, the first part being penned in 1883 and the fourth part completed in 1885. When Nietzsche started writing this work, he had recently lost his 'family' of Lou Salomé and Paul Rée, and he now, more than ever, felt alone in the world. Zarathustra is about solitude and the hero of the book is the loneliest of men. Zarathustra the prophet has returned with a new teaching, having realized the 'error' of his old prophecy.

The book is written in a biblical style, with a narrative, characters, events, setting and plot. In these respects, it is very different from Nietzsche's other works and helps to explain its more popular appeal.

Case study: Zarathustra

Zarathustra was a prophet, a historical figure also known by the name the Greeks gave him, 'Zoroaster'. The dates of his life are uncertain: he is thought to have lived at any time time between the eighteenth and sixth centuries BCE. Zoroastrianism was the official religion of the mighty Persian Empire for around a thousand years, and small groups of Zoroastrians still exist in Iran and among the Parsis in India.

Zarathustra is regarded as the author of the religious texts known as the *Gathas*, which consist of 17 hymns. Some of these hymns are devoted to singing the praises of Ahura Mazda, the highest deity, while others are autobiographical, describing the prophet's mission to promote the teaching of Ahura Mazda, only to be ignored – leading the prophet to doubt that he was the right one for such a mission. These autobiographical hymns must have particularly inspired Nietzsche's Zarathustra, who has similar experiences bringing a 'new teaching'. Equally, Nietzsche would have been sympathetic towards the prophet's emphasis on the individual's own responsibility for his or her destiny and freedom to choose right or wrong.

Zorastrianism also influenced Greek philosophy, especially that of the Presocratic thinker Heraclitus, who inspired Nietzsche's own thoughts, as he says in *Ecce Homo*:

> *'I have not been asked, as I should have been asked, what the name Zarathustra means in precisely my mouth, in the mouth of the first immoralist ... Zarathustra was the first to see in the struggle between good and evil the actual wheel in the working of things: the translation of morality into the realm of metaphysics, as force, cause, end-in-itself... Zarathustra created this most fateful of errors, morality: consequently he must also be the first to recognize it... His teaching, and his alone, upholds truthfulness as the supreme virtue – that is to say, the opposite of the cowardice of the "idealist", who takes flight in face of reality; Zarathustra has more courage in him than all other thinkers put together.'*
>
> Ecce Homo, 'Why I Am Destiny', 3

A brief summary of *Thus Spoke Zarathustra*

The Zarathustra of the Persians was the first prophet to talk of the Day of Judgement, of time reaching a final end. However, Nietzsche's Zarathustra provides a very different teaching.

At first choosing solitude in the mountains, Zarathustra grows weary of his own company and descends to seek companions and to teach his new philosophy. But, even when surrounded by disciples, he retreats once more to his solitude and praises its virtues. The new teaching that Zarathustra presents is based upon the foundation that God is dead, and, subsequent to this, the teachings on (and striving to become) the Superman, the will to power and the eternal recurrence.

PART I

> '"All gods are dead: now we want the Superman to live" – let this be our last will one day at the great noontide'.
> *Thus Spoke Zarathustra*, 'Of the Bestowing Virtue'

Zarathustra descends from the mountains after ten years of solitude and expresses the need for a new teaching to replace the old teaching of a belief in God and morality. The new teaching, 'God is dead', will be brought by another teacher: not Zarathustra, but a 'Superman'. However, the masses laugh at Zarathustra and so he sets out to find followers. In this first part, it is Zarathustra who perhaps learns more, rather than actually teaches, as he realizes that concepts such as the Superman cannot easily be taught. It is not enough simply to tell the people about the Superman through a series of statements. By the end of Part I, he has instead gathered together a small band of disciples rather than attempt to preach to the masses. It is a realization on the part of Zarathustra – and Nietzsche, too – that his words are not for Everyman.

PART II

> *'I go new ways, a new speech has come to me; like all creators, I have grown weary of the old tongues. My spirit no longer wants to walk on worn-out soles.'*
>
> Thus Spoke Zarathustra, 'The Child and the Mirror'

Having told his disciples to leave him and to find their own way, Zarathustra now looks within himself for enlightenment, returning once more to the mountains. After the passing of years, Zarathustra once again descends among his disciples with a 'new speech'. In the section 'Of Self-overcoming', he talks of the will to power and states that the highest human beings, those who know how to utilize the will to power in the most positive sense, are philosophers. These philosophers, these Supermen, will destroy the values that people have cherished and replace them with new values. They will teach humankind how to love the earth.

PART III

> *'Behold, we know what you teach: that all things recur eternally and we ourselves with them, and that we have already existed an infinite number of times before and all things with us.'*
>
> Thus Spoke Zarathustra, 'The Convalescent'

This part acts as the climax for the previous two parts. Zarathustra separates from his disciples and takes a long sea voyage, for he no longer needs disciples. In solitude once more, Zarathustra wills for eternal recurrence, for his 'redemption'.

Spotlight

Writing Part III, for Nietzsche, was, he reported, the happiest time of his life. For Nietzsche, writing was a form of therapy, but also he believed that reading his works could be therapeutic for the reader. Philosophy as therapy may seem a relatively new idea, but it was something Nietzsche acknowledged.

PART IV

In this part, Zarathustra's solitude is broken by a series of visitors, including a soothsayer, two kings, a scholar, a sorcerer, the last Pope who also believes that God is dead, the 'ugliest man', the beggar and Zarathustra's own shadow. Zarathustra has a 'last supper' with his visitors, preceded by a speech about the Superman. He then engages in question-and-answer conversation on such issues as the Superman and the death of God.

Part IV deals with a major concern of Nietzsche: redemption. In *The Birth of Tragedy*, Nietzsche argued that humankind could be redeemed through the revival of Greek tragedy and the renewal of German culture. However, as he became disillusioned with the possibilities of Art to achieve this, Nietzsche still avoided the pessimistic response and believed that there still can be redemption, that there is still a need to revalue all values and overcome decadence. However, Part IV is less naive, as the ironic realization dawns that affirming life can be achieved only by resenting life as it presently is.

Spotlight

Nietzsche had originally intended Part III to be the final one. When he wrote a fourth part he distributed it to only around 20 people and it was not added to the book until 1892, when Nietzsche had gone insane and was in no position to object to its conclusion. Many scholars have argued that *Zarathustra* is a better book without the fourth part. However, although the work is certainly more consistent with only the first three parts, the fourth part is very important in terms of understanding Nietzsche's development as a philosopher.

The eternal recurrence

A central theme of *Thus Spoke Zarathustra* is the eternal recurrence. In fact, for Zarathustra, embracing the concept was, for him, salvation. What did Nietzsche mean by this? This doctrine of the eternal recurrence only gets a few mentions in his later works, although Nietzsche does hint at it in *The Gay Science*, where he presents a 'what if' image. He asks: What if a demon were to creep up to you one night when you are all alone and feeling lonely and were to say to you that the life you have lived and continue to live will be the same life you will live again and again for infinity? This life will be exactly the same: no additions and no omissions, every pain, every joy, every small and great event. If this were the case, would you cry out in despair over such a prospect, or would you think it to be the most wonderful outlook ever?

Though not mentioned specifically, this 'what if' scenario sums up the eternal recurrence: whatever in fact happens has happened an infinite number of times in exactly the same detail and will continue to do so for eternity. You have lived your life an infinite number of times in the past and will do so an infinite number of times in the future.

Importantly, like, seemingly, the doctrine of the will to power, Nietzsche presents the eternal recurrence as a thought experiment, not a provable truth. You do not have to believe the demon is telling the truth, merely to consider the prospect of it being true and the psychological effect this has upon you. Consider the possibility yourself: does it make you happy or fill you with despair? Like the will to power, the aim is to provide an insight into the way we live our lives and, perhaps, even to change the way we live our lives. If indeed we experience despair at the prospect of living this life again and again, then it logically follows that we are not happy with the way we live our lives.

Nietzsche considered that merely thinking of the possibility was the greatest of thoughts and would have an impact on how you perceive yourself and how you live the rest of your life. This is why he gave it such central importance in *Zarathustra*. Proof of the doctrine is not important here; it is sufficient to consider it as simply a possibility. Nietzsche's aim in presenting the eternal recurrence was to present a positive doctrine of an 'afterlife' – one that would not devalue this life. In this way, it is much more powerful than the religious view of Heaven. The Christian view of the afterlife, Nietzsche thought, acts as a consolation and causes people to accept their lot in this life with the prospect of a better life when they die (provided they are not destined for Hell, of course!).

Nietzsche was not original in presenting the idea of the eternal recurrence. In his *Untimely Meditations,* he had criticized the doctrine of eternal recurrence that existed in the ancient Greek philosophy of Pythagoras. Nietzsche's criticism of it at that time was that events do not and cannot recur within the span of known history. If Nietzsche did not accept eternal recurrence as understood by Pythagorean philosophy, then can we speculate over what he did mean by it? Apart from the ancient Greek philosophers, Nietzsche came across the theory in a more contemporary sense in a writer he much admired, the great German poet Heinrich Heine (1797–1856). In one of his works, Heine refers to time being infinite whereas the things in time – concrete bodies – are finite. He then speculates that if this is the case, given an infinite amount of time, the atoms that have dispersed will eventually reform exactly as before. Therefore, we will be born again in the same form. However, the real impetus for the eternal recurrence was Schopenhauer, who considered it to be the most terrible idea possible, an image of endless suffering.

Is this some basis for Nietzsche's belief in the eternal recurrence? The reader must be reminded that, as with the will to power, Nietzsche was not primarily setting out to prove his doctrine, yet, also like the will to power, it is important to consider the problems with it and what foundational basis, if any, there can be for such a doctrine. Although Nietzsche did not present a proof in his published writings, he wrote a great deal about it in his notes. However, in making use of Nietzsche's notes, we need to be very careful and not equate the idle and often careless scribbling with what Nietzsche was prepared to present as the final work. It is largely because Nietzsche's sister, Elisabeth, proceeded to publish his notes after he went insane that people accepted them as his own philosophy, which led to a misunderstanding of his ideas.

Bearing this cautionary note in mind, Nietzsche's own speculations on the doctrine can be presented as a useful intellectual exercise. Taken from his notes, we can summarize an attempt at a proof as a series of premises with a conclusion:

1 The sum total of energy in the universe is infinite.

2 The number of states of energy is finite.

3 Energy is conserved.

4 Time is infinite.

5 Energy has infinite duration.

This summary bears a strong resemblance to Heine. We can see what Nietzsche is getting at here: it is rather like the classic example of a monkey in front of a typewriter who, given an infinite amount of time, will eventually write the complete works of Shakespeare. The monkey is typing away in a random manner but, in time, the correct combination of letters will be achieved. Likewise, the states of energy are random but, given an infinite amount of time, will reconstitute themselves.

However, there are a number of problems with this:

▶ Nietzsche relies upon two basic assumptions: that time is infinite (it has no beginning or end) and that the 'states of energy', the matter of the universe, are finite. These, of course, are assumptions that may not in fact be the case and are yet to be proven one way or the other. Much of modern cosmology argues that the universe began with a 'Big Bang' and does have a limited timespan; however, it is anybody's guess what existed before the Big Bang or what will occur once this universe ceases to exist.

▶ It may well be the case that you would live this life again and again for infinity, but this would not motivate you to live this life to the full because, if such a theory were true, it would also mean that every conceivable combination of events would also occur. You can imagine the worst life possible:

the most miserable, deprived and painful existence that you could live, and you will live it again and again, no matter what you do in this life. Nietzsche can only get around this by accepting a deterministic view that not all possible combinations can occur, only a return of those combinations that have actually occurred in human history. On this issue, Nietzsche does seem to present both possibilities in his notes.

▷ Georg Simmel presented an elegant rejection of the view that states must recombine given an infinite amount of time. Imagine three wheels of the same size rotating on the same axis. On the circumference of each wheel a mark is placed so that all three wheels are aligned. The wheels are then rotated, but at different speeds. If the second wheel is rotated at twice the speed of the first and the third wheel was $1/\Pi$ of the speed of the first, the original alignment would never recur, no matter how much time elapsed. Nietzsche, however, may retort that his 'states of energy' are random, whereas Simmel's wheels maintain a constant speed. If they ran at random speeds, then they would eventually realign.

It is curious that Nietzsche places greater emphasis on this doctrine in his notes and letters than any other aspect of his philosophy, and yet he never elaborated upon it in his published works. When we consider what was important for Nietzsche, what stands out is his belief throughout his life that existence should be justified; that is, the true philosopher does not go through life happily in an unquestioning manner, but seeks to give meaning and value to his existence. In *The Birth of Tragedy*, Nietzsche thought life could be justified, could have value, through art – or rather 'Art' in the ancient Greek sense. The Greeks lived a life of 'Dionysian joy'. However, Nietzsche, later in life, felt that Art was not the salvation he had originally hoped and it was in August 1881, while walking in the Swiss mountains, that the thought came to him of the eternal recurrence. With this thought came an experience, a psychological impact that caused him to affirm life and to love it.

This feeling of joy, Nietzsche thought, is the formula for the greatness of the human being, and he is making an essential connection with the doctrine of the Superman. The Superman is one who, like Zarathustra, is able to embrace the doctrine of eternal recurrence and find redemption within it. If, before and after every action, you were to ask, 'Do you want this action to occur again and again for all eternity?' and you could answer in the joyful affirmative, you are exercising the will to power in a positive manner. The weak look to the next life for hope, whereas the strong look to this life.

It is important always to keep in mind what was happening at the time Nietzsche was writing. The rise of nihilism was a serious concern for Nietzsche and he was only too aware of the political implications of such beliefs – or lack of beliefs – for the future of Europe.

Spotlight

The concept of the eternal recurrence – or eternal return – has been used in a number of films, including the 1993 Hollywood romcom *Groundhog Day*, which tells the story of Phil Connors (played by Bill Murray) who wakes up every morning at the same time (2 February, Groundhog Day) in the same place and experiences the same events.

Zarathustra and the Superman

In *Thus Spoke Zarathustra*, the prophet descends from his mountain to teach the Superman. The German word Nietzsche used is *Übermensch*, which literally translates as 'Overman'. However, 'Superman' – despite the comic-book connotations and the possibility of misleading people into believing in some superhuman figure – remains a common translation. Nietzsche did not invent the term, and would have come across it in the works of the great German poet Goethe (1749–1832) and, in his study as a classical philologist, in the works of the Greek writer Lucian of Samosata (*c*.120–80 CE). However, it was Nietzsche who gave the term a new meaning.

In *The Gay Science*, Nietzsche uses the term *Übermensch* to refer to gods and heroes of, especially, the ancient Greeks. For him, these were symbols of nonconformity, of those who did not fit within the norm but were prepared to challenge contemporary values and beliefs. This is a theme – the stress on individualism and the realization of one's self – evident in Nietzsche's earlier works, and a careful reading of these shows the development of his thought previous to the first appearance of the Nietzschean Superman in *Thus Spoke Zarathustra*.

In the second of his *Untimely Meditations*, for example, Nietzsche talks about the goal of humanity, and that this must rest with its highest specimens. That is, Nietzsche is aware of what humankind is capable of achieving and raises the question of why we usually fail to live up to our potential. There are examples in history of great people, of philosophers, artists and saints, but even they remain 'human, all too human'.

Nietzsche often sings the praises of Napoleon, not because of his military prowess but because he represents what Nietzsche calls the 'good European'; the person who is not obsessed with the kind of nationalism that was plaguing Germany at the time of Nietzsche. In this arena, Nietzsche also places such figures as Goethe, Beethoven, Caesar and Michelangelo. However, none of these is a 'Superman', but each represents certain features that make up the will to power, such as self-mastery, individualism and charisma. Nonetheless, in the end all of these figures still remain 'human, all too human', for Nietzsche is quick to recognize their faults. There has never been a Superman, although Nietzsche sees the ideal as a Caesar with the soul of Christ. Even Zarathustra is only the herald of the Superman, not one himself.

Importantly, the link with the eternal recurrence is that the Superman is one who will embrace the doctrine: who can look to his own life and wish to relive it again and again for infinity. It is an unconditional acceptance of existence, a saying 'Yes' to everything. For Nietzsche, the Superman is an affirmation of life – the opposite of Schopenhauer's denial of it and a desire for the self to be extinguished.

However, it is one thing to talk of a Superman, of the highest specimen, of greatness, but what does this greatness really mean in terms of our values? Much of Nietzsche's writings have been taken out of context, and none more so than his references to the Superman and a super race. By the Superman, Nietzsche did *not* mean some blond giant dominating and persecuting lesser mortals. Nietzsche's sister Elisabeth helped to promote the idea that he did, and she also assured Hitler that it was he whom her brother had in mind when he talked of the Superman. Nietzsche talked of a new direction, but a new direction towards what? What are the political, moral and practical applications?

An understanding of the will to power and eternal recurrence gives us some indication, but to understand what Nietzsche meant by the Superman we need to consider his later work.

After *Zarathustra*

It is evident from his notes and letters that the ideas in *Thus Spoke Zarathustra* had preoccupied Nietzsche for some time. After its completion, Nietzsche felt exuberant. Although rarely mentioned by name in his works, the hypothesis of the will to power was always there in the background and the theme was developed to some extent in the works to come, which proved to be his finest. These were *Beyond Good and Evil* (1886), *On the Genealogy of Morals* (1887) and *Twilight of the Idols* (written in 1888 and published in 1889). It was a prolific and original period in Nietzsche's life during which he gradually abandoned the aphoristic style in favour of a more coherent form.

Spotlight

It was during this period that Nietzsche was as 'settled' as he would ever be. He had established a routine of spending the summers in Sils-Maria and the winters in Nice. (Nice had had been an Italian city (Nizza) before 1860, when it was ceded to Napoleon III's French Empire, though Nietzsche always refused to recognize it as French.) He had got over the Rée–Salomé affair and he now reduced his contact with the outside world to a bare minimum, concentrating on his writing. His health continued to worsen, however, to the extent that he was now nearly blind. The fact that he continued to write so prolifically is a credit to his own will to power.

Much of *Zarathustra* was written in Nice, where Nietzsche's health always took a turn for the better, but the summer of 1884 in Sils-Maria proved less pleasant. He had trouble sleeping and said that, when he closed his eyes, he would see an array of flowers. He feared that he was going mad, but this may well have been due to his consumption of drugs, including hashish, and alcohol, which included stout and pale ale.

Nietzsche insisted that everything he wrote after *Thus Spoke Zarathustra* was a commentary upon it. However, the Superman is not mentioned again, the eternal recurrence only occasionally crops up, and the will to power remains, mostly, below the surface. Perhaps it is an exaggeration to say that his post-Zarathustra works are merely 'commentaries': they are works of philosophy in their own right and introduce many new ideas and concepts. At the same time, they do help to explain and elaborate upon the concepts previously introduced, especially his next book, *Beyond Good and Evil*.

Nihilism

One of the stated aims of *Beyond Good and Evil* was to liberate Nietzsche's Europe from what he considered to be a decline into decadence, nationalism and stupidity. His concerns for the future of Europe turned out to be prophetic, of course, and this helps us understand why Nietzsche himself was often taken to be something of a prophet after his death – an image his sister Elisabeth was more than happy to promote. The title *Beyond Good and Evil* can be misleading, because it suggests that we must cast aside all values, that there are no values and, consequently, the coming of the Superman heralds a breed that can do as it pleases, without any regard or concern for others. This, however, is not what Nietzsche meant to express.

In a desire to give it some kind of label, some critics have described Nietzsche's philosophy as **nihilism**, from the Latin *nihil*, meaning 'nothing' and suggesting negativity and emptiness, a rejection of all values and a belief in nothing. Yet Nietzsche could be a very positive, joyful and affirmative philosopher.

We can categorize two types of nihilism, neither of which Nietzsche falls into but was nonetheless influenced by: Oriental nihilism and European nihilism.

ORIENTAL NIHILISM

Schopenhauer was heavily influenced by what he understood of Buddhist teachings and, when he talks of extinguishing the self and that the world we live in has no ultimate reality, it is this form of nihilism that he is considering. It possesses the following characteristics:

▶ Because the world we live in is not real, our attachment to it is an illusion.

▶ Life is without sense or point, merely an endless cycle of birth and rebirth.

▶ To find salvation, we must escape from this world and extinguish the concept of the self.

EUROPEAN NIHILISM

The Russian author Ivan Turgenev (1818–83) was the first to introduce the nihilist to the novel. In his greatest novel, *Fathers and Sons* (1862), the hero is Bazarov, an idealistic young radical dedicated to universal freedom but destined for tragedy. This novel reflected a nihilism that existed in the latter decades of nineteenth-century Europe:

▶ Nihilists consisted mostly of the younger generation, who rejected the beliefs and values of the older generation.

▶ Rejecting the beliefs of their elders about religion, tradition and culture, these nihilists claimed to believe in 'nothing'.

▶ However, the nihilists replaced traditional beliefs with a belief in science. Instead of seeking salvation in the next life, the nihilists looked to a better understanding of this world as the future hope.

THE 'NIHILISM' OF NIETZSCHE

In both Oriental nihilism and European nihilism, there still exists a belief in salvation – that there can be a form of order and values. Nietzsche, however, goes much further than this:

▶ All belief systems, whether in the field of science, religion, art or morality, are fictions. They are merely instances of the will to power.

▶ This world is the only world, even if it is valueless. There is no 'unity', no 'truth'.

▶ This fact should not lead to pessimism, to a 'will to nothingness'. Rather, we should adopt a Dionysian 'yes' to life.

To say that the world is 'valueless' is not to say that it has little worth. Rather, it does not make sense to say one thing has more 'value' than another, because there is no such thing as a scale of values. Nothing has value; there are no facts, no 'better' or 'worse'. This was a rejection of the belief of so many philosophies and religions that there is an objective world. These religions and other metaphysical propositions often endorse a **correspondence theory of truth** (see also Chapter 8). This theory holds that when we use terms like 'God', or 'good' or 'bad' or 'justice', we are making reference to an actual 'God', an actual 'justice' and so on; that is, these terms correspond to a reality. For Nietzsche, there is no reality for these terms to correspond to. Nietzsche's views on truth and perspectivism are considered in the next chapter.

Amor fati: love your fate!

For European nihilism, especially of the Russian variety, a rejection of traditional values had political implications with the call for a revolution. Nietzsche's main concern, however, was with the psychological impact of the acceptance that there are no truths. He saw that it could well lead to pessimism and despair or the attitude that 'anything goes'. Nietzsche viewed nihilism as a positive affirmation of life and as freedom from the burden of hope in an afterlife, in salvation. You should love your fate without the need of fictions and false securities to comfort you.

Nietzsche's 'nihilism' finds its culmination in the doctrine of the eternal recurrence. Man must not only accept his fate and, indeed, love his fate, but also embrace this purposeless existence as recurring again and again for infinity. The person who can do this deserves the title 'Superman':

- The Superman rejects the belief that there are objective values or values of any kind.

- The Superman does not, as a result, become a pessimist or suffer from despair; rather, he embraces life and loves his fate (*amor fati*).

- Even when faced with the prospect that he will have to live exactly the same life again, the Superman's *amor fati* is not dented. Even existence in its most fearful form is a joyful one.

Nietzsche has presented us with a picture of humanity and its relation to the world it lives in. This picture is of a people constantly trying to impose an order, structure and meaning upon a universe that has no order, structure or meaning. Rather, the universe is in a state of constant change, plurality, chaos and becoming. There is no benign God, there are no objective moral values, there is no, in Kantian terms, 'noumena'.

Nietzsche asks why, for probably the whole history of humanity, we have clung on to beliefs in God or objective values. Obviously, we have a need for religious and metaphysical comfort but, as Nietzsche's world approached the twentieth century, there was a growing feeling that such beliefs no longer had intellectual credibility. A belief in God was filled with too many paradoxes and contradictions, too many claims to truth that conflicted with the evidence.

As more and more people began to question religious claims, they looked for other 'truths' through science, through art, or through Kantian metaphysics. Yet, for Nietzsche, this was just replacing one fiction with another. Having said that, during his earlier writings, notably in *The Birth of Tragedy*, Nietzsche attributed value to art. Nietzsche recognized that art can help give meaning to life and help us access a different way of understanding the world. Although Nietzsche recognized the psychological benefits of art, it was another thing to believe that art is any 'truer' than any other belief. This is not something that Nietzsche would subscribe to.

Nietzsche always took an interest in science, too. He recognized that science provided humanity with many benefits. Whereas religion was concerned with the next life, with salvation and the eternal soul, science at least provided knowledge of the world that might endure the scepticism of generations. Here, however, we can see some contradictions in Nietzsche's own thinking for, at times, his emphasis upon science seems to go against his own view that there are no 'facts'. But, although impressed with the methods of scientific investigation, later in life he adopted the view that science, too, rested on errors. Science, like art, is creation and invention rather than discovery, for there is nothing there to discover. Undoubtedly science is useful, but this is different from believing that science is true. This realization, that all beliefs are simply a matter of perspective, is the first step that must be made if man is to overcome man.

Key ideas

Amor fati: Latin for 'love your fate', a term Nietzsche used to express an affirmation of life

Correspondence theory of truth: the view that, when we talk of things being 'true', we are referring to things that actually exist in reality: when you point to an object and say 'it is there', then it really is there

Eternal recurrence: the teaching that this exact life has occurred an infinite number of times in the past, and will continue to do so an infinite number of times in the future

Nihilism: literally a 'belief in nothing'; there are varying levels of nihilism: at its less extreme it is a rejection of contemporary values and traditions, but does present the possibility of alternatives

Orientalist: a term used to describe Western writings, paintings and other cultural artefacts that present a romantic and distorted picture of the East, or the 'Orient'

Übermensch: a German word that literally translates as 'Overman' but that is usually translated as 'Superman' when referring to those prepared to question accepted beliefs, assert their individuality and embrace the idea of eternal recurrence

Things to remember

▷ *Thus Spoke Zarathustra* is Nietzsche's most popular work. It develops the themes of the will to power, the Superman and the eternal recurrence.

▷ Nietzsche's character of Zarathustra is to some extent autobiographical and can be seen as Nietzsche heralding the coming of the Superman.

▷ The principal idea of the eternal recurrence is that whatever in fact happens has happened an infinite number of times in exactly the same detail and will do so for eternity. Nietzsche did not set out to prove the doctrine of the eternal recurrence; rather to present it as a thought experiment and to challenge us to consider what our reaction would be if the doctrine were true.

▷ The Superman is someone prepared to embrace the doctrine of eternal recurrence and to look forward to the possibility of living his or her life over and over for ever.

▷ Although the term 'Superman' is the usual translation of the German *Übermensch*, this does not imply a superhuman being. Rather, it requires humanity to adopt a certain psychological stance towards the world and to consider the possibility of adopting new values.

▷ Nietzsche's nihilism was not a belief in 'nothing' and the resulting view that 'anything goes'. Rather, it is a rejection that there are objective values of any kind.

▷ Nietzsche adopted the stance of *amor fati* – that you should love your own fate and embrace the doctrine of eternal recurrence.

Fact-check

1 Who, historically, was Zarathustra?
   a A Greek god
   b A Persian prophet
   c A biblical prophet
   d A Persian king

2 What is the title of Nietzsche's book featuring Zarathustra?
   a *Beyond Zarathustra*
   b *The Good and Evil of Zarathustra*
   c *Thus Spoke Zarathustra*
   d *Zarathustra the Superman*

3 What does the term *amor fati* mean?
   a Love your fate
   b Love your faith
   c Love your fat
   d Fast in the morning

4 What is the literal translation of *Übermensch*?
   a Underman
   b Overman
   c Other man
   d After man

5 What is the correspondence theory of truth?
   a Sending letters to other people reveals truths about them
   b Terms we use do not correspond to reality
   c Terms we use do correspond to reality
   d The words we use are meaningless

6 Which of the following best describes a nihilist?
   a Someone who likes to list things
   b Someone who has faith in God
   c Someone who wants to blow up things
   d Someone who rejects contemporary values

7 Which of the following best describes an Orientalist?

    a Someone who presents a romantic, distorted image of the East

    b Someone who likes to travel to Asian countries

    c Someone who collects antiques from the East

    d Someone who was born in the East

8 In which one of the following did Nietzsche read about eternal recurrence?

    a Heinrich Heine

    b William Shakespeare

    c Johann von Goethe

    d William Wordsworth

9 In which one of the following did Nietzsche read of the *Übermensch*?

    a Heinrich Heine

    b William Shakespeare

    c Johann von Goethe

    d William Wordsworth

10 Which one of the following is *not* a Nietzschean doctrine?

    a Will to power

    b Eternal recurrence

    c *Übermensch*

    d Nihilism

Dig deeper

Douglas Burnham and Martin Jessighausen, *Nietzsche's* Thus Spoke Zarathustra: *An Edinburgh Philosophical Guide* (Edinburgh: Edinburgh University Press, 2010)

Clancy Martin and Daw-Nay Evans, *Nietzsche's 'Thus Spoke Zarathustra': A Reader's Guide* (London: Continuum, 2014)

Friedrich Nietzsche, *Thus Spoke Zarathustra*, trans. by R.J. Hollingdale (London: Penguin, 1974)

Laurence Lampert, *Nietzsche's Teaching: An Interpretation of 'Thus Spoke Zarathustra'* (New Haven: Yale University Press, 1989)

On truth and perspectivism

In this chapter you will learn:

▶ *what Nietzsche means by 'truth'*
▶ *about his use of the term 'perspectivism'*
▶ *about the value he placed on reason and on language.*

Imagine you are staring at a painting, and that this painting represents the sum of all life and experience. The painting, you might think, is finished. The paint is dry and it hangs upon the wall. For Nietzsche, however, this is not a finished painting – it is still evolving and it will continue to evolve for ever.

Most people accept 'common sense': that there is a world out there, that when you kick a stone there is an actual stone, that the laws and behaviour so embedded within our lives are so real that they are not questioned. (The painting is thick with paint and it is difficult to wipe aside the colours and shapes of earlier generations.)

For Nietzsche, however, our 'common sense' is merely an interpretation. This is Nietzsche's **perspectivism**: we see the world from our own accumulated lives and experiences, but this does not make it right. The painting is not an accurate representation of something 'out there', but the imaginings of the human mind.

The theory of knowledge

'Granted that this is only interpretation – and you will be eager enough to make this objection? – well, so much the better.'

Beyond Good and Evil, 22

One important field of philosophy is known as **epistemology**, or the theory of knowledge. A number of philosophers would argue that this field is the most important one for philosophers to enter: what can we know with any certainty? The word 'philosopher' is from the Greek 'lover of wisdom' and, while the term 'wisdom' seems to be rarely used these days to describe knowledge, the primary task of philosophers is the same, and it goes right back to the Greeks who asked the questions that still engage us today. How 'wise' can we be? That is, how much can we know and what do we mean when we say we 'know' something to be the case?

For example, someone may feel inclined to make a seemingly innocent remark such as 'the sky is very blue today'. The philosophical response to this would be to raise questions concerning the validity of the statement 'the sky is very blue today'. Is the sky very blue for everybody? When we say it is blue, what colour are we perceiving in our heads? Is the sky itself actually blue or do we only see it as blue? What is meant by very blue as opposed to just blue? How blue can blue be? Would the sky be blue if there was no one around to see it? Can we really know for sure what colour the sky actually is? And so on! In fact, the last question gets to the heart of epistemology. We are unable to step outside our own bodies. We cannot 'see' the world as it actually is because we see it via our senses. Can we always trust our senses?

Case study: varieties of truth

It might seem odd to talk about 'varieties' of truth, for surely there is just truth. But philosophers have presented a number of different understandings of truth. There is absolute truth (something is true absolutely under any circumstances); contingent truth (the truth is dependent upon place, time and so on); necessary truth (given a set of statements, something has to be true and cannot be otherwise); scientific truth; mathematical truth; relative truth and so on. However, most philosophical understanding of truth can be divided into two: the correspondence theory of truth and the coherence theory of truth.

The correspondence theory of truth

This is the most common notion of truth. This asks whether a proposition actually corresponds to something in the real world. For example, if someone says 'that car is red' while pointing to a red car, then that statement corresponds to a reality. If, at the time, they are actually pointing to a brown dog, then it can be shown that the statement does not correspond. Effectively, the correspondence theory states that there is a relation between statements of belief ('that car is red') and the actual state of affairs (there is an actual red car there). Its attraction is in its intuitive appeal, but Nietzsche sets out to attack this theory especially.

The coherence theory of truth

This evaluates the truth of statements by relating them to other proven truths within a system of thought. It might help to conceive of truth as a web of beliefs: those beliefs at the centre of the web are the most enduring, such as the belief that other people exist, that we all have to die some day, that the sun gives heat and light and so on. The further we go from the centre of the web, the less solid and permanent are our beliefs. Some beliefs that were central may drift to the edges but, so long as they fit together, the web remains intact. If a belief is so inconsistent with our other beliefs, it is so far on the outskirts of the web as to be ignored by most, or rejected altogether. In this view, there may be no claims to absolute truths, only their coherence.

Nietzsche's perspectivism

'What then in the last resort are the truths of mankind? They are the irrefutable errors of mankind.'

The Gay Science, 265

Nietzsche would not deny that we *want* truth; he states in *The Genealogy of Morals* and elsewhere that we *will* truth. However, if we look for Truth in an objective sense, with a capital 'T', it involves turning our back on this life and looking for something 'out there' – something that, for Nietzsche, does not exist in any comprehensible way. It is therefore a pointless exercise and also detrimental for humanity because of its deflection from this life. Whatever knowledge we have is always from a perspective and this fact is unavoidable. Even though the world we experience is shaped by our own perception and perspective, and it has no more substance than a supposed 'other world', it is nonetheless the one we are able to live in.

Nietzsche's perspectivism raises more questions than it answers because Nietzsche does not really go out of his way to explain in any detail what he means by perspectivism. For example, are there groups of perspectives such as the religious perspective or the scientific perspective, or are there individual perspectives so that each person has a different perspective from everyone else?

One important point that Nietzsche makes in, for example, *The Anti-Christ*, is worth stressing: 'truth and the belief that something is true: two completely diverse worlds of interest' (*AC*, 23). In other words, a perspective is not the same as a belief or a set of beliefs; to say 'I believe the sky is very blue today' is not the same as having a perspective. Nietzsche is being much more radical than that, but if it isn't a belief then what is it? Nietzsche, to put it bluntly, does not help us out here.

It may help to go back to one of Nietzsche's earlier works, an essay called 'Of Truth and Lies in a Non-moral Sense', written just a year after *The Birth of Tragedy* but not published during his lifetime. In this work, Nietzsche looked at Greek culture through 'the perspective of life' rather than from any kind of absolute standpoint, and here we already have the germ of Nietzsche's perspectivism – that it is simply impossible to see things from a 'perspectiveless perspective'. In the essay, Nietzsche says that there is a generally accepted way of seeing things. For example, in morality, it is generally considered that lying is bad and telling the truth is good. But from the 'perspective of life' things can look different: weaker people often preserve themselves by lying, cheating, flattering, deceiving and so on. So from that perspective – the perspective of surviving – lying can be seen as a positive thing.

The influence of Kant can be seen here in the sense that Nietzsche acknowledged that human beings can only know things from a human perspective, but Nietzsche went much further than Kant in denying that there is a single human perspective. Rather, there are many different human perspectives depending upon time, place, group, physiology, environmental conditions, stronger and weaker types, and so on.

'In fact all tables of values – all "you ought tos" – which we know from history or ethnological research, in any case, first require a physiological examination and interpretive explication, before even a psychological one; similarly, all of them stand in need of a critique from the side of medical science.'

On The Genealogy of Morals, Essay 1, Section 17

Common sense – the acceptance that things are how we think they are – is not only seen as necessary for life, but also useful. Nietzsche would not disagree with this. Our 'painting' of the world is not a random collection of colours and shapes, but a purposeful process of understanding the world and adapting to it; that is, our world view is necessary for our very survival. To this extent, common sense is true in that it allows us to function.

This understanding of truth is equated with utility: how useful is a particular interpretation of the world? By declaring that God is dead, Nietzsche is stating that the belief in God no longer serves a useful purpose. Nietzsche's 'nihilism', then, is not a rejection of common sense; it is not the discarding of a painting that has taken generations to construct. To discard it would not only be foolhardy but impractical. Rather, Nietzsche's nihilism is a rejection of common sense being really true in any objective sense – that it is perfect, immutable and complete.

Truth, therefore, is an evolving process. This may suggest a pragmatic theory of truth in his rejection of the belief in God, and it is understandable that a number of scholars have suggested this, but Nietzsche remains ambiguous. While he generally accepts that what is true has been throughout history equated with what is stable, reliable and workable, this is not to say that Nietzsche himself therefore accepts these things as true in a pragmatic sense, especially as his interest in health requires himself at least to be unpragmatic and prefer falsehoods. At the same time, it could be argued that Nietzsche is being pragmatic here in advocating health as life-enhancing.

Also, at times, Nietzsche can be quite dismissive of illusions because they do not represent what is really true. In *Human, All Too Human*, Nietzsche speculated that there might indeed be a metaphysical world, but at the very best this is just a bare possibility and so it would be much too inadequate to look to it for salvation.

Here, however, there seems an inconsistency in Nietzsche's thought: is there a real world or isn't there? Truth, for Nietzsche, seems to be equated with workable fictions, yet he also seems to want to say what the world is actually like. Here he becomes muddled, on the one hand declaring that the world is a matter of perspective, while on the other not entirely denying the possibility that we can have endurable facts. As an example, it is a fact that humans need oxygen to breathe. Are we to say that this is a matter merely of perspective, a truth that we need to survive but that we cannot say that there really is oxygen, and we really need it? Are we then presented with a hierarchy of knowledge, in which some things are more true than others? Even if Nietzsche were to say, as he seems to, that our understanding of the world all boils down to aspects of the will to power, he would run the danger here of introducing his own metaphysics: a force that prevails across the universe.

Spotlight

It is difficult to appreciate Nietzsche's epistemology without having some background understanding of the views of previous philosophers. In particular, the reader would gain much by having some knowledge of, especially, Hume's empiricism and Kant's response to this.

Reason and the senses

Not only was Nietzsche frequently labelled a nihilist but he was also called an anti-rationalist. Nietzsche, however, was not against reason. What he was against was anything that is not useful, anything that makes life impossible. His criticism was not against reason, but against rationalist philosophers such as Plato. Plato emphasized reason at the expense of the senses and this world. His rationalism took him into another realm, a belief in rational truth. As a result, Plato considered this world an illusion and a distraction from rational meditation.

The senses can give us grounds for belief, but never true knowledge. Nietzsche held that reason couldn't be accepted at the expense or neglect of the senses. Even in his later work *The Twilight of the Idols* (1889), Nietzsche continues to hold that the senses allow us to sharpen our beliefs and teach us to think. Nietzsche here is not being irrational in an emotive, animal sense. Although he also believed that the passions are important and that they can teach us, he saw the senses as an educative tool that enables us to observe the world and fine-tune our perspective of it.

Spotlight

Nietzsche cannot be so easily 'pigeonholed' when it comes to ascribing his views on knowledge. Sometimes he seems to come close to Hume's empiricism, while at other times he resembles Kant. Perhaps the best approach is to see his perspectivism as uniquely Nietzschean.

The importance of language

Nietzsche was one of the first philosophers to appreciate the importance of language in the construction of our beliefs. This needs to be borne in mind when Nietzsche himself uses such words as 'soul', 'truth' and so on.

The Austrian philosopher Ludwig Wittgenstein (1889–1951) famously stated that, 'The limits of my language mean the limits of my world.' If we consider the history of thought, we become aware that this history is almost entirely full of a belief in gods, a God, an afterlife and the eternal soul. It is only very recently, representing a small fraction of the timeline of human history, that people have begun to question these concepts. Returning to our painting once more: if every brushstroke represents a century in the history of humankind, the questioning of metaphysical concepts amounts to only one such brushstroke, hidden among thousands of others. If our world view is painted in such a way, Nietzsche asserted that so, also, is our language. In *Twilight of the Idols*, Nietzsche famously declared that we would not get rid of God until we get rid of grammar. The British philosopher Bertrand Russell (1872–1970) later echoed this view: he believed that everyday language embodies the metaphysics of the Stone Age. If we are to establish a better philosophy, then we must work out a new language.

Spotlight

In 1929 Wittgenstein arrived at Cambridge to take up a post as lecturer and fellow. By this time, he was already a famous philosopher. However, he did not have a Ph.D. and so could not be a real don. He agreed to submit his great work *Tractatus* as his

Nietzsche argues that the language we speak seduces people. When people use terms such as 'mind' or 'soul', it is so embedded within our language that, as Nietzsche says, we would rather break a bone in our body than break a word. Most of our language is based upon humankind's early use of language, upon a more primitive psychology that we therefore cannot escape from because of our use of everyday language. When we use a word, we still remain attached to the common-sense view that the word actually refers to something, rather than it being the product of humankind many generations ago.

'What, then, is truth? A manoeuvrable army of metaphors, metonymies, anthropomorphisms – in short, a summation of human relationships which have been poetically and rhetorically heightened, transposed, and embellished, and which, after long use by a people, are considered to be solid, canonical, and binding: truths are illusions whose true nature has been forgotten.'
'Of Truth and Lies in a Non-moral Sense'

Our attachment to our language is so strong that we could not readily do without the fictions it describes. Nietzsche also believed that even the language of physics is a fiction, an interpretation to suit us. He talks of the concept of atoms as a useful tool to explain the nature of the universe, but that is all that they are. However, Nietzsche's perspectivism goes much further than this, for it is not just theoretical entities such as atoms but all entities that are fictions. All bodies, lines, surfaces, concepts of cause and effect and of motion; these are all just articles of faith but do not in themselves constitute a proof.

Nietzsche asks why it is necessary to believe in such concepts as cause and effect. He does not entirely accept the Kantian view that we have 'human spectacles' and that we therefore have no choice but to perceive the world in a certain way. Rather, we have learned through harsh experience that the way we perceive the world is the most suitable for survival. There may well have been many people who have seen the world in a different way but, as a consequence, have perished. The view of causality that Nietzsche presents is not very different from David Hume's. Hume argued that we arrive at the concept of cause and effect not because causality actually exists in nature, but because, through habit, we conjoin one event with another. Therefore, causality is a product of the mind, but a necessary product nonetheless. For Nietzsche, they are conventional fictions that are useful for communication.

There have been philosophers and scientists who have also rejected the world of common sense, but Nietzsche asserts that they then make the mistake of creating another world that they consider to be real. Despite Nietzsche's charity towards science, he does not accept that it has brought us any closer to reality because, for Nietzsche, there is no reality to get close to. Since the time of Galileo in the seventeenth century it has been the practice of scientists to present theories that conflict with the contemporary common-sense view of the world, such as the view that the earth revolves around the sun or that humanity evolved from other species. This has resulted in often-radical transformations in our understanding of the world and led to a new common-sense view. For the scientist, these theories are usually regarded as allowing us to get closer to how the universe really is. For Nietzsche, despite their pragmatic application, they are still nonetheless a fiction. They are no more real than the previous world view.

Nietzsche could never persuade himself to adopt the absolute idealist stance that there is no world outside the mind. This is because he believed, like Kant, that there is a world out there, but a world so different, so unwilling to be tied to our desire for an ordered and structured universe, that it is impossible to even so much as conceive of this world, let alone talk about it. Nietzsche, therefore, does not entirely escape from Kant's clutches. As he grew older, Nietzsche speculated more about this real world. Inevitably, however, as soon as one attempts to talk about the real world we are immediately tongue-tied by the limitations of our language. Because we have no other language, we are sucked into using metaphysical terms that tie us to our world view.

Although we may not have any other language, we can perhaps play with language. Certainly, Nietzsche's aphoristic style, his clever play on words and his confrontational and controversial idioms, force us to question and think. Not unlike mystical traditions that employ poetry, riddle, koans and so on, in an attempt to describe the indescribable, Nietzsche is also compelled to use similar methods. This may well give his philosophy a mystical quality, but perhaps this is unavoidable.

Spotlight

Nietzsche is not a sceptic about knowledge, although – rather like Hume – he may be considered an 'academic sceptic': someone who in an academic context is sceptical about whether we can really know anything with certainty, but nonetheless on an everyday basis (outside academia) lives life on the assumption that certain things are 'true'.

Does Nietzsche's perspectivism help to provide us with a clearer understanding of the Superman? Nietzsche's *Übermensch* would not be deluded into believing in a reality that can be attained or comprehended, nor would he look to religion or philosophy for salvation. He would be less concerned with stating what is true than in telling what is false, yet he would also need to be tied to a common-sense perspective if he were to survive; the extreme sceptic would not be able to get out of bed in the mornings. However, this should not prevent daring experimentation in seeking a new language and philosophy. Would Nietzsche go so far as to suggest a physical change also? Is he pre-empting the advances in genetic engineering? This, one suspects, would be giving the German philosopher too much credit.

Key ideas

Coherence theory of truth: the view that beliefs are considered 'true' to the extent that they cohere with other beliefs, although there may be no absolute truths

Correspondence theory of truth: the view that when we talk of things being 'true', we are referring to things that actually exist in reality; when you point to an object and say 'it is there', then it really is there.

Epistemology: the branch of philosophy concerned with the nature and scope of what we can know

Perspectivism: the view that we perceive the world according to our perspective, although this may not be as the world actually is

Pragmatic theory of truth: the opposite of the 'correspondence theory of truth' – something is only 'true' to the extent that it is practical to believe in it

Things to remember

▶ Epistemology is the theory of knowledge. In philosophy, it is the study of what we can know, and what we mean by 'knowledge'.

▶ Nietzsche is critical of the correspondence theory of truth: that statements about things actually correspond to things in the real world.

▶ Nietzsche is perhaps closer to the coherence theory of truth – that truths are 'true' so long as they cohere – but even this does not entirely describe Nietzsche's perspectivism.

▶ Nietzsche's perspectivism is that we see the world from a collection of perspectives, although these do not necessarily correspond to how the world actually is.

▶ Nietzsche's nihilism is not a rejection of common sense as such, but rather a refusal to accept that common sense is 'true' (i.e. that it corresponds to the way the world is).

▶ Nietzsche is not an anti-rationalist, but he is critical of the view that only reason can provide us with a true picture of the world.

▶ For Nietzsche, we are 'seduced' by our language and to change our beliefs we also need to change what we mean by our words.

▶ Nietzsche is not an idealist (in the philosophical meaning of the term) but he does not go so far as Kant in asserting that there are 'noumena'.

▶ Nietzsche may be a philosophical sceptic, but he also accepts that we need 'workable fictions' in order to survive.

Fact-check

1 What does the term 'epistemology' mean?
- **a** Theory of knowledge
- **b** Theory of art
- **c** Theory of life
- **d** Theory of love

2 Which one of the following is a definition of the correspondence theory of truth?
- **a** A statement is 'true' to the extent that it coheres with other beliefs
- **b** A statement is 'true' to the extent that it refers to an actual state of affairs
- **c** A statement is true if someone says it is true
- **d** There are no true statements

3 Which one of the following is a definition of the coherence theory of truth?
- **a** A statement is 'true' to the extent that it coheres with other beliefs
- **b** A statement is 'true' to the extent that it refers to an actual state of affairs
- **c** A statement is true if someone says it is true
- **d** There are no true statements

4 Which one of the following best describes Nietzsche's views?
- **a** Nihilist
- **b** Anti-rationalist
- **c** Perspectivist
- **d** Rationalist

5 Which one of the following would not be called a philosopher?
- **a** David Hume
- **b** Ludwig Wittgenstein
- **c** Bertrand Russell
- **d** John Maynard Keynes

6 Who said, 'The limits of my language mean the limits of my world'?

    a David Hume

    b Ludwig Wittgenstein

    c Bertrand Russell

    d John Maynard Keynes

7 Which one of the following is not a work by Nietzsche?

    a *Beyond Good and Evil*

    b *Twilight of the Idols*

    c *On Truth and Perspectivism*

    d 'Of Truth and Lies in a Non-moral Sense'

8 Which of the following best describes the attitude of Nietzsche's Superman?

    a Someone so sceptical about knowledge as to be unable to function

    b Someone who would not seek for ultimate truth, but would adopt a common-sense perspective

    c Someone who would embrace God as truth

    d Someone who would look to science for all the answers

Dig deeper

Steven Hales and Rex Welshon, *Nietzsche's Perspectivism* (Champaign, IL: University of Illinois Press, 2010)

Friedrich Nietzsche, 'Of Truth and Lies in a Non-moral Sense' (available in various editions and translations)

Peter Vardy, *What is Truth?* (New South Wales: UNSW Press, 1999)

9

Nietzsche and religion

In this chapter you will learn:

▶ *about Nietzsche's 'religiosity'*

▶ *the effect his Lutheran upbringing had on his philosophy*

▶ *about Nietzsche's 'religious experience'*

▶ *why Nietzsche valued religion*

▶ *about the importance of myth*

▶ *about the role of religion in the state*

▶ *about Nietzsche and Islam*

▶ *about Nietzsche and Buddhism.*

Nietzsche has often been described as an atheist, and his declaration 'God is dead' would seem to support such a view. Yet an essential appeal of his philosophy is his use of religious language, metaphors and symbols; in addition, Nietzsche did not escape entirely from his Lutheran upbringing. Further, Nietzsche was specifically addressing an audience at a specific time and place (that is, the coming new century in Europe) and what Nietzsche perceived to be an important turning point for Europe: the dawn of a new age in which the old God was dead and society was confronted with increasing secularization. An understanding of Nietzsche's 'religiosity' needs to be seen within the context of his lack of faith in the secular order to provide humanity with any meaningful existence.

This chapter explores how Nietzsche's Lutheran background influenced his views about God and religion – Islam and Buddhism as well as Christianity. It also looks at other key themes: his criticism of modernity and his idea of the philosopher-king.

Nietzsche's religiosity

'I have a terrible fear I shall one day be pronounced holy... I do not want to be a saint, rather even a buffoon.'

Ecce Homo, 'Why I Am Destiny', 1

Some scholars of the past have acknowledged that Nietzsche has religiosity. For example, the German philosopher Martin Heidegger (1889–1976) called him 'that passionate seeker after God and the last German philosopher'. More recently, the British essayist Erich Heller (1911–90) said of him: 'He is, by the very texture of his soul and mind, one of the most radically religious natures that the nineteenth century brought forth...'

More recent writers such as Alistair Kee and Giles Fraser have argued that Nietzsche is very much a religious philosopher, as summed up in the following quotes:

Nietzsche as a 'sort' of atheist

Nietzsche may not be an atheist in a traditional sense because, while not believing in God, he at the same time was not lacking in religiosity. At the very least, Nietzsche did declare himself a devotee of the Greek god Dionysus and Nietzsche's Lutheran upbringing cannot be totally disregarded. Although Nietzsche may not be concerned with the existence or otherwise of God – and does not bother to engage in any of the standard arguments for or against the existence of God – he nonetheless deals with, in the words of the theologian Paul Tillich, what is of 'ultimate concern': how are we to be 'saved'? By 'saved' this need not require the baggage of theological teachings related to salvation, for it is enough to conceive salvation as a concern for the future of the human race on this earth. Nietzsche's concern is to replace what he perceived as a pathologically sick belief in a Christian God with a new life-affirming framework for salvation.

An important reason why Nietzsche uses Christian imagery and ideas, even though 'God is dead', is that the death of God does not bring theology to an end, rather to a fresh beginning: the death of God is what makes salvation possible. In *Twilight of the Idols*, Nietzsche remarks, 'We deny God; in denying God we deny accountability: only by doing that do we redeem the world.' To do this, Nietzsche reaches for Christian imagery.

Nietzsche the Lutheran

'It was only out of the soil of the German Reformation that there could grow a Nietzsche.'
Dietrich Bonhoeffer, *Ethics* (Norwich: SCM Press1955), p. 71

A number of factors contribute to Nietzsche's religious outlook: the tight-knit Lutheran background, the influence of his father – a pastor – his piety as a child, the key places of his upbringing all being at the geographical centre of Lutheranism, and enrolment to study theology at the University of Bonn. In fact, Nietzsche saw Luther as one of his heroes up until the time he split with Wagner, and Nietzsche is deeply indebted to Lutheran Pietism, the movement that was prevalent in the time and place of Nietzsche's upbringing. Pietism is essentially anti-rationalist, indifferent to theological speculation and concerned more with instinct – with engaging with Christ on a personal rather than an intellectual level. This emphasis upon instinct is central to Nietzsche's philosophy, as this quote from *The Anti-Christ* highlights:

'It is false to the point of absurdity to see in a "belief"... the distinguishing characteristic of the Christian: only Christian practice, a life such as he who died on the Cross lived, is Christian... Even today such a life is possible, for certain men even necessary: genuine primitive Christianity will be possible at all times... Not a belief but a doing...'
The Anti-Christ, 33

Nietzsche is not of course against rationalism as such (see Chapter 8), but he considered it more important to trust your instincts and to be led by your passions. He wrote to his friend Peter Gast: 'I have a taste, but it rests upon no reasons, no logic, and no imperative.' In the case of religion, it is our 'taste' that decides whether we engage with it or not, rather than reason. Nietzsche's pietism has been associated with his *amor fati* (see Chapter 7): to hate life is blasphemous.

While Nietzsche has been called a nihilist, Nietzsche himself sees Christianity as nihilistic, as life denying and depraved, in which life can have meaning only by reference to some otherworldly realm. With the death of God, this nihilism is unmasked and Europe is faced with apparent hopelessness, devoid of salvation. At this point – the point which Nietzsche believed existed in Europe during his time, the post-moral period – Nietzsche sees the opportunity to address the question of whether humanity really needs redemption from the divine: cannot human life be self-affirming? Throughout Nietzsche's philosophy there is a sense of urgency, a recognition that there existed in his time a very brief window of opportunity. He believed that the power of *ressentiment*, of self-hatred (a potent use of the will to power), would quickly regroup under another guise with new prophets. One reason why Nietzsche is so widely read today must be due to the recognition that these new salvations have come under such brands as communism, nationalism, capitalism and other '-isms'.

Salvation, for Nietzsche, is an internal transcendence. It is a healing process to cure humanity of what he saw as a disease brought about by attempts to ameliorate suffering through Christian redemption. However, rather than healing, Christianity has made the patient worse. Nietzsche's conception of health is not that of a pain-free state, for he believed pain to be a prerequisite of health. Nietzsche believed that Christianity does not cure, it anaesthetizes: it blocks pain and persuades people that the absence of pain is the same as salvation.

Nietzsche and 'inspiration'

Mention has already been made of Nietzsche's curious 'religious' experience beside the lake of Silvaplana (see Chapter 3). In *Ecce Homo*, Nietzsche again refers to this experience: 'It was on these two walks that the whole of the first Zarathustra came to me, above all Zarathustra himself, as a type: more accurately, *he stole up on me...*' (*EH*, Thus Spoke Zarathustra, 1) and, in the same book, Nietzsche says the following:

> *'If one had the slightest residue of superstition left in one, one would hardly be able to set aside the idea that one is merely incarnation, merely mouthpiece, merely medium of overwhelming forces. The concept of revelation, in the sense that something suddenly, with unspeakable certainty and subtlety, becomes visible, audible, simply describes the fact. One hears, one does not seek; one takes, one does not ask who gives; a thought flashes up like lightning, with necessity, unfalteringly formed – I have never had any choice. An ecstasy whose tremendous tension sometimes discharges itself in a flood of tears, while one's steps now involuntarily rush along, now involuntarily lag; a complete being outside oneself with the distinct consciousness of a multitude of subtle shudders and trickling down to one's toes... Everything is in the highest degree involuntary but takes place as in a tempest of a feeling of freedom, of absoluteness, of power, of divinity.'*
>
> Ecce Homo, Thus Spoke Zarathustra, 3

Such remarks do not suggest a man who lacks a religious outlook. This 'inspiration' is not conceived of in terms of ideas that Nietzsche himself invented, but rather it comes across as a mystical feeling 'of power, of divinity'.

Religion as life enhancing

For Nietzsche, it is not important whether religion is true or not, but whether or not it is life enhancing. Perhaps the best way to understand Nietzsche is not as a global philosopher full of grand schemes, but as a local philosopher. When reading Nietzsche it is better to think locally – to find out what his specific target is. For example, Nietzsche does not reject compassion wholesale, but rather compassion that leads to nihilistic ends. He does not attack compassion and self-sacrifice as such – in fact, Nietzsche was considered a compassionate person by those who knew him – but how it is expressed through such individuals as Schopenhauer and Paul Rée. It is interesting that both Schopenhauer and Rée, like Nietzsche in certain respects, were atheists, determinists and naturalists, yet Nietzsche goes out of his way to condemn them.

Does he reject the belief in the supernatural, the non-empirical? No. Rather, he is concerned with what is achieved as a result of a belief. For example, the belief in Greek gods is quite acceptable because it signified an affirmation of life. Therefore, certain kinds of religion, of the supernatural, are equally acceptable. A future society could indeed be supernatural and non-empirical.

When Nietzsche writes about religion, when he is either being critical of Christianity or positive about Christ, Buddhism or Islam, his ultimate value is health: what promotes greater health? What he means by this, in a seemingly Freudian sense (and perhaps even a Platonic one), is that our selves – our 'souls' if you will (and Nietzsche himself freely uses the word 'soul') – are fragmented. Humans are, for the most part, fragmented with drives all over the place.

On Islam

Interestingly, Nietzsche makes over a hundred references to Islam and Islamic cultures in his works. At times, he pours great praise on Islam, with his admiration of the people in general and in particular for individuals such as the Muslim Sufi poet Hafiz (1315–90). He talks of the great achievements of Muslim Spain, and sees Islam as a life-affirming religion in opposition to the life-denying Christianity of his time. At the same time, Nietzsche can come across as incredibly ignorant and **Orientalist** (see Chapter 7) in his perception of Islam and the Islamic world, which he shared with many Europeans at this time, who saw Islam as a manipulative instrument of social engineering and the Prophet Muhammad as a cunning impostor. Nietzsche read many Orientalist texts, including those by William Palgrave, Julius Wellhausen and Max Muller.

Case study: Muhammad Iqbal

The Indian scholar and poet Muhammad Iqbal (1873–1938) received a classical, Western education as a boy at the Scotch Mission College in Sialkot (in the Punjab province of what is now Pakistan, but which was part of India at that time). In 1905 he travelled to Europe and studied at Cambridge before travelling on to Heidelberg and Munich to obtain his doctorate entitled 'The Development of Metaphysics in Persia'. In a way that many of his Muslim predecessors had looked to ancient Greek and Persian philosophers, Iqbal made use of his studies of Western philosophy, especially that of Nietzsche, to inform his understanding of Islam. Certainly, a Nietzschean influence can be detected, especially in his first collection of poems, *Secrets of the Self*, which he published in 1915.

Iqbal saw Nietzsche's Zarathustra and, more generally, the concept of the *Übermensch*, as possessing the characteristics of the Prophet Muhammad in Islam. Like Nietzsche's Zarathustra, Iqbal sees Muhammad as the archetype for a politics of redemption: one who founded a new metaphysics of morals that consisted of courage and honesty; one who cast aside false idols. Iqbal sees the Prophet Muhammad as confronting the human predicament of the time in seventh-century Arabia (and Mecca especially), a time of nihilism, in the same way that Zarathustra was confronted by the death of God and the consequent failure to have a belief in any moral values to replace divine guidance. In *Secrets of the Self*, the 'self' smells suicide in conventionalism and this life of decadence, and regards this as the same as no life at all.

Iqbal argues that the role of the prophets, whether it is Zarathustra or Muhammad, is to be a destroyer of conventional values and to create new values. On a number of occasions in the notes from the composition of *Thus Spoke Zarathustra*, Nietzsche portrays Zarathustra as a lawgiver (*Gesetzgeber*), ranking him alongside Buddha, Moses, Jesus and Muhammad. Whereas Nietzsche looked to Zarathustra as a response to what he saw as a moral decline, Iqbal looked to the example of the Prophet Muhammad as an example of how Muslims should respond to what Iqbal saw as a moral decline among Muslims in the nineteenth century.

Leaving aside the contradictory nature of his remarks, the fact that Nietzsche feels so ready to make any remarks at all concerning Islam and its culture is interesting in itself. One scholar, Ian Almond, states that Nietzsche's sympathy and interest in Islam may well be a result of his distaste for German culture. That is to say, Nietzsche exaggerates the features of an 'other' culture in order to demean his own. This cultural claustrophobia, leading to a longing for the Orient, is not new, especially among Romantic poets (for Nietzsche, these were Heinrich Heine and Goethe). Nietzsche never actually visited a Muslim country and his access to sources on Islam would have been, on the whole, Orientalist in their perspective.

In a sense, Nietzsche's Orientalism and the question of how correctly this represents Islam was irrelevant so far as Nietzsche is concerned. What matters to him is how useful it is. This comes back to Nietzsche's perspectivism, considered in Chapter 8. What this suggests is that Nietzsche was not so much interested in Islam and Islamic culture as such and, for that matter, was not that learned in it either, but rather he used it as a battering ram against his own culture. In addition, Islam served an epistemological function by highlighting the weaknesses of European culture, and so presenting possible alternatives. Importantly, the appeal of Islam for Nietzsche was that he perceived it as less modern, less democratic, less enlightened and hence much better, given his criticism of so-called enlightened, democratic Europe. As Nietzsche himself said, 'I want to live among Muslims for a good long time, especially where their faith is most devout: in this way I expect to hone my appraisement and my eye for all that is European.'

An example of Nietzsche's perspective on Islam is his admiration for the Assassins: this group, the Hasishin, was an outcrop of the Ismaili Shi'a sect and existed from around the eleventh to the thirteenth century. Their primary task seemed to be to engage in being the medieval equivalent of suicide bombers, particularly assassinating rulers whom they considered to be corrupt and oppressive. Nietzsche was not condoning political assassination here: rather it has to do with Nietzsche's fascination with the Other. And the more seemingly 'Other' the better – his fascination lies with extremities of difference, something that is reflected in one letter to his sister Elisabeth, when he states that he wishes to live in Japan simply because it is so radically different from his own European culture, rather than because he has any particular affinities with Japanese culture as such.

The following quote from Section 60 of *The Anti-Christ* illustrates this:

'Christianity robbed us of the harvest of the culture of the ancient world, it later went on to rob us of the harvest of the culture of Islam. The wonderful Moorish cultural world of Spain, more closely related to us at bottom, speaking more directly to our senses and taste, than Greece and Rome, was trampled down (I do not say by what kind of feet): why? because it was noble, because it owed its origin to manly instincts, because it said Yes to life even in the rare and exquisite treasures of Moorish life!... Later on, the Crusaders fought against something they would have done better to lie down in the dust before – a culture compared with which even our nineteenth century may well think itself very impoverished and very "late"...'

The Anti-Christ, 60

Here Nietzsche declares Muslims to be 'one of us', and his view of Islamic culture as being closer than that of ancient Greece and Rome is quite remarkable considering Nietzsche's own Hellenic leanings.

Myth, modernity and monumental history

Spotlight

Why is Nietzsche so popular today? To a great extent, his criticisms of modernity were ahead of their time and it is only in recent years, following some of the negative effects of modernity – heavy industrialization, a struggle to find meaning, global warming and so on – that we can relate to what Nietzsche was saying more than a century ago.

If we are looking for recurrent themes in Nietzsche, then undoubtedly a key theme is his criticism of **modernity**, of the way we are now. This theme has occurred in Nietzsche's writings right from his first major work, *The Birth of Tragedy*. The term 'modernity' is a much-bandied one, and is considered to be the result of two important revolutions: the French Revolution and the Industrial Revolution. Henry Cox refers to the 'five pillars' of modernity as:

1 the emergence of sovereign national states

2 hegemony of science-based technology

3 bureaucratic rationalism

4 profit maximization as a prime motivator

5 secularization.

For Nietzsche, in monumental history we have, and we need, role models that inspire us to greatness through imitation. For monumental figures to be monumental they must be mythologized, not deconstructed and individualized. Our heroes need to be lacking specific detail, to be blurred around the edges, so that we can fill the gaps with our poetic invention. That is, they have to be flexible in order to be relevant to our modern times. A healthy, thriving culture, for Nietzsche, is one that possesses the 'plastic power' to 'incorporate... what is past and foreign', to 'recreate the moulds' of the past in the language of the present (*UM*, II, 1). In a sense, the mythologized figures act as our unwritten laws for a community. Only monumental history is creative, although that is not to say that you should not also be critical. To flourish, Nietzsche says, 'man must possess and from time to time employ the strength to break up and dissolve a part of the past.' How we are to judge this is on the basis of what is life fulfilling, what makes us grow. Nietzsche is critical of the Christianity of his time because it poisons life; this is in contrast to his praise of Jesus as a monumental, mythical figure.

Nietzsche argued that history, as it now serves in the world of modernity, atomizes. Historical events are merely historical facts, a vast encyclopedia or, in more modern terms, a

Wikipedia. Modernity lacks culture, it is a 'fairground motley', a 'chaotic jumble' of confused and different styles (*UM*, I, 1). In Nietzsche's *Thus Spoke Zarathustra*, the prophet both loves and scorns the town known as 'Motley Cow' because its citizens are cow- (herd-)like and yet live in a chaotic jumble of different lifestyles.

This is reminiscent of Plato's criticism of democracy: lots of bright colours but nothing solid or certain. Culture, therefore, represents a unity of the people, a *Volk*. Nietzsche argues that presenting us with a smorgasbord of lifestyle options that have no evaluative ranking produces a mood of confusion and cynicism. Rather than taking part in life, we become spectators. There is, granted, elitism here, for example, in the often quoted: 'Mankind must work continually at the production of individual great men – that and nothing else is its task' (*UM*, III, 6). Humankind needs to create favourable conditions for great men to thrive, as a plant thrives in the right soil. Note the similarity with Plato's views on the need for the right kind of society if the philosopher-king is to flourish. But this should not be interpreted as calling for a society where the elite few bask in glory while the many live in the sewers. Nietzsche, rather, is calling for a gradual revolution in which the characteristics of the 'higher' (more adaptive) type become the norm rather than the exception, and so the great individual is not an end in itself – that would be pointless – but rather a means to the redemptive evolution of a whole community. We need leadership; we need role models.

Religion and the state

The next chapter will consider in some detail Nietzsche's political views (and, indeed, whether Nietzsche has any political views) but here it is worth considering the role of religion in any political order proposed by Nietzsche. His views on religion are closely tied with the coming of the Supermen, of the philosophers of the future. These philosophers will possess the virtues of courage, nobility and an ability to face cruel reality rather than hide behind the 'cowardice' of false idealism:

> 'I deny first a type of man who has hitherto counted as the highest, the good, the benevolent, beneficent; I deny secondly a kind of morality which has come to be accepted and to dominate as morality in itself – décadence morality, in more palpable terms Christian morality.'
>
> Ecce Homo, 'Why I Am Destiny', 4

Zoroaster is the first prophet to claim that salvation can be obtained through moral behaviour. Thus personal responsibility comes to the forefront: one will be judged on the Day of Judgement. Time is perceived as linear, moving morally towards its final consummation in the struggle between good and evil. Nietzsche recognizes the Abrahamic tradition of prophetic religions that appeal to an authority higher than the ancestral or the civil, but he would argue that they originate much further back than that: to the work of Zarathustra. This understanding of history is very perceptive: the recognition that Hebrew prophets would have been influenced by Zoroastrian, as well as Greek, thought, during their period of exile. On many occasions in the notes from the composition of Zarathustra, Nietzsche portrays Zarathustra as a lawgiver (*Gesetzgeber*), ranking him alongside Buddha, Moses, Jesus and Muhammad.

Nietzsche, as we shall see in the next chapter, is critical of democracy and the secularization of political authority. As he says in *Human, All Too Human*, 'In the sphere of higher culture there will always have to be sovereign authority, to be sure – but this sovereign authority will hereafter lie in the hands of the oligarchs of the spirit.' What is needed to cure social ills 'is not forcible redistribution of property but a gradual transformation of mind: the sense of justice must grow greater in everyone and the instinct for violence weaker.' The capacity to build a new future depends on an ability to see a continuity with the strength of past traditions. An important passage in *Human, All Too Human* called 'Religion and Government' notes that the importance of religion in the life of a culture is that it consoles the hearts of individuals in times of loss, deprivation and fear; that is, in times when a government is powerless to alleviate the sufferings of people during such tragedies as famine and war. However, the increase in democracy has seen a parallel decline in the importance of religion.

Beyond Good and Evil is particularly enlightening when it comes to determining Nietzsche's views on the role of religion. The oligarchs of the spirit in the quote above in *Human, All Too Human* are referred to again in *Beyond Good and Evil*. What is needed, he argues, is a new spiritual aristocracy that is 'strong enough and original enough to give impetus to opposing value judgements and to revalue, to reverse "eternal values"' (BGE, 203). Nietzsche's hierarchical society will have a place for religion, for it legitimizes the power of rulers and generates obedience, as well as providing comfort for the hardship of those who are ruled. Yet Nietzsche, of course, is not subscribing to Christianity or any other religion of his time, so what would this religion be?

'...the one I was just speaking about; and he has come again and again, the god Dionysus, no less, that great ambiguous tempter god, to whom, as you know, I once offered my first-born [Birth of Tragedy] in all secrecy and reverence.'
Beyond Good and Evil, 295

Dionysus is both life-affirming and satisfies the metaphysical need; a need Nietzsche acknowledges and which is something that modernity cannot offer. All modernity can offer is scepticism, relativism and nihilism.

On Buddhism

Much of Nietzsche's comments on religion were levelled at Christianity, but, as we have seen, Nietzsche was also interested in Islam and its culture. Another religion that attracted his curiosity was Buddhism. As with Islam, Nietzsche is much kinder to Buddhism than he is to Christianity, for it lacks what is at the core of Christianity: *ressentiment*.

It should not come as too much of a surprise that Nietzsche talks about Buddhism, as his early enthusiasm for Schopenhauer would have made him aware of the influence of Eastern religions on Schopenhauer's philosophy, particularly the emphasis on the eradication of suffering and the world as nothing but illusion. But, like his knowledge of Islam, Nietzsche had a very narrow understanding of Buddhism, which he saw through the eyes of a select number of German scholars rather than through first-hand experience or reading the works of Buddhist thinkers from the Eastern tradition. However, no doubt one appeal of Buddhism for Nietzsche is that there is no omnipotent God with the accompanying doctrines on redemption, sin, grace, a separate world and so on. Consequently, there is no need for prayer or public displays of faith, no need for richly decorated churches and an elitist priestly class:

> 'Buddhism is a hundred times more realistic than Christianity – it has the heritage of a cool and objective posing of problems in its composition, it arrives after a philosophical movement lasting hundreds of years; the concept "God" is already abolished by the time it arrives. Buddhism is the only really positivistic religion history has to show us, even in its epistemology (a strict phenomenalism), it no longer speaks of "the struggle against sin" but, quite in accordance with actuality, "the struggle against suffering".'
>
> The Anti-Christ, 20

For Nietzsche, Buddhism is 'positivistic' in that it is more scientific and more in accordance with 'reality'. Rather than emphasize sin, Buddhism focuses on suffering, which, again, appealed to Nietzsche, for suffering seemed more immediately to be a condition of human nature than sin. As Buddhists do not have the guilt of sin, they are beyond the hatred and envy that is *ressentiment*. Instead, they talk of moderation and benevolence. In addition, because Buddhism has arisen 'after a philosophical movement lasting hundreds of years', Nietzsche considers it to be a more mature, more philosophical religion.

However, Nietzsche still regards Buddhism as a 'decadent' religion and, therefore, no more than one step on the path of nihilism. One key topic that Nietzsche disagreed with is the Buddhist view that suffering stems from desire, and so the only way we can get rid of suffering is through a regimen of mental and physical activities, to get rid of desire. While Nietzsche agrees that suffering is central to human nature and that it is caused by desire, he does not agree that we should therefore get rid of desire, for to do so would be to turn us into inhuman, robot-like, passionless people. What makes us human is our suffering. To eliminate desire would not only be wrong and inhuman, but in actual fact impossible if humans are to continue to exist at all.

Key ideas

Modernity: a period in history represented by intellectual, cultural and economic movements such as industrialization, secularization and the nation-state; a complex and multifaceted phenomenon

Secularization: the transformation of a society away from an identification with religious values towards non-religious values and institutions

Things to remember

▶ It is inaccurate to describe Nietzsche as an atheist, at least in the sense of being entirely irreligious. In many respects, he was a very spiritual person who appreciated the importance and value of religious belief.

▶ Nietzsche's criticism is of a particular form of religion, specifically Christianity as it existed at the time.

▶ For Nietzsche, it is not important whether religion is true or not, but whether or not it is life-enhancing.

▶ Nietzsche is often highly complimentary of Islam, although more with the intention of contrasting it with Christianity than with praising its beliefs per se.

▶ A key theme in all of Nietzsche's writings is his criticism of modernity.

▶ He recognized the importance of religion within the state, provided it is the 'right kind' of religion.

▶ He was also more praising of Buddhism than he was of Christianity – he saw the former as more philosophical and not so subject to such symptoms as *ressentiment*.

Fact-check

1 Of which Greek god did Nietzsche declare himself to be a devotee?
   a Zeus
   b Aphrodite
   c Dionysus
   d Hermes

2 Which of the following intellectual movements was Nietzsche especially critical of?
   a Dadaism
   b Communism
   c The Reformation
   d Modernism

3 To which religion does Nietzsche make over a hundred references in his writings?
   a Islam
   b Hinduism
   c Sikhism
   d Scientology

4 Why was Nietzsche more positive towards Buddhism than he was towards Christianity?
   a Because it lacks *ressentiment*
   b Because he liked to meditate
   c Because the Buddha was an example of Nietzsche's *Übermensch*
   d Because Nietzsche had travelled to many Buddhist countries

5 Who described Nietzsche as 'that passionate seeker after God and the last German philosopher'?
   a Wagner
   b Hegel
   c Heidegger
   d Freud

6 Which Sufi poet did Nietzsche admire?
- **a** Hafiz
- **b** Rumi
- **c** Jami
- **d** Nurbakhsh

7 Why was Nietzsche so interested in Islam?
- **a** He had lived and travelled in many Islamic countries
- **b** Some of his best friends were Muslims
- **c** He saw it as a contrast to Western culture
- **d** He had considered converting to Islam

8 Which particular Islamic group did Nietzsche admire?
- **a** The Wahhabis
- **b** The Assassins
- **c** The Shi'a
- **d** The Ismailis

Dig deeper

Giles Fraser, *Redeeming Nietzsche: On the Piety of Unbelief* (London: Routledge, 2002)

Lucy Huskinson, *The SPCK Introduction to Nietzsche: His Religious Thought* (London: SPCK, 2009)

Roy Jackson, *Nietzsche and Islam* (London: Routledge, 2007)

Alistair Kee, *Nietzsche against the Crucified* (Norwich: SCM Press, 2009)

Robert Morrison, *Nietzsche and Buddhism: A Study in Nihilism and Ironic Affinities* (Oxford: OUP, 1999)

10
Nietzsche and politics

In this chapter you will learn:

▶ *about Nietzsche's criticisms of democracy*
▶ *what it means to call Nietzsche an 'immoralist'*
▶ *about his views on slavery*
▶ *about his views on women*
▶ *whether Nietzsche actually has any firm political views in his writings.*

While one important modern debate in academic circles among Nietzschean scholars is whether or not he can be considered an ethical naturalist, another fascinating clash of views is on whether or not Nietzsche subscribes to any political views and, if so, what they are. Some scholars have argued that Nietzsche has no political ideals in his writings whatsoever and so to devote a whole chapter to Nietzsche's political views could be construed as way off the mark. However, many other scholars do argue for a political Nietzsche.

This chapter discusses Nietzsche's views on society and politics, outlining his arguments for a hierarchical society and his critical view of democracy, which he saw as a hindrance to culture. For him, an elite would benefit society as a whole, and the top of the pyramid would be his philosophers of the future, his oligarchs of the spirit.

On democracy

> 'I am not a man I am dynamite... Only after me will there be grand politics *on earth.'*
> Ecce Homo, 'Why I Am Destiny', 1

While Nietzsche is a great admirer of Athenian culture, the same cannot be said of that other great Athenian invention: democracy. Rather than support the view held by some – that Athenian culture was a result of democracy – Nietzsche praises the flourishing of the arts in Athens *despite* its democracy, seeing it as more of a hindrance to culture than a benefactor. In fact, it seems that Nietzsche's dislike for democracy goes back a long way: he resigned from a student fraternity because he disapproved of what he regarded as a democratic admissions policy. Already, in his student years, he was a man displaying elitist tendencies even before he had developed any strong philosophical views.

One point that needs to be borne in mind was that at the time Nietzsche was writing, democracy was something of a 'new idea', despite its origins – though in a rather different form than we know it today – in ancient Greece. Much of Europe at the time was fundamentally aristocratic, and so the view of democracy would have been very different from what, today, is largely taken for granted and considered by many as the best form of government. Having said that, more egalitarian views were certainly being bandied around during his time, not least from his friend Wagner, who argued for the abolition of the state and the introduction of radical egalitarianism. In addition, Meysenbug was also a campaigner for democracy and was exiled because of it.

The Birth of Tragedy was originally intended to involve a discussion of politics and it does seem odd that Nietzsche omitted this. What was to be part of the book became a separate essay called 'The Greek State'. This interesting essay is often ignored by scholars, which is a shame as it shows quite clearly that Nietzsche not only had an interest in politics but was also quite familiar with political theory – perhaps not surprisingly, given the company he kept. The crux of Nietzsche's argument against democracy (as well as feminism, socialism and anarchism) is that it is merely a continuation of Christianity: an ethics of equality that weakens the strong and preserves the failures. He believed that, in such a political climate, culture would find it difficult to flourish.

'The Greek State' is a work of cultural criticism, particularly aimed at the contemporary phenomenon of modernity (see previous chapter) with its atomized individualism and such egalitarian themes as the dignity of man and the dignity of labour.

The ancient Greeks, on the other hand, recognized that a life devoted to labour makes it impossible to create great art. Wagner argued that Greek culture could not be revived because it deserved to perish. Why? Because it was founded upon slavery and so any culturally fulfilled society of the future must exist without slavery, including wage slavery, which, of course, was characteristic of the capitalism that was emerging at the time. Nietzsche, however, in his typically contentious manner, argues that slavery is an essential feature of any society that wishes to attain high culture. Slavery is the essence of culture:

> 'If culture really rested upon the will of the people, if here inexorable powers did not rule, powers which are law and barrier to the individual, then the contempt for culture, the glorification of poorness in spirit, the iconoclastic annihilation of artistic claims would be more than an insurrection of the suppressed masses against drone-like individuals; it would be the cry of compassion tearing down the walls of culture; the desire for justice, for the equalization of suffering, would swamp all other ideas.'
>
> 'The Greek State', p. 7

Here Nietzsche is presenting us with a choice: you can have democracy with its smorgasbord of lifestyle options that have no evaluative ranking, thus producing a mood of confusion and cynicism, or you can have aristocracy with its higher states of being, its Supermen.

Comparisons can be reasonably made between Plato's conception of the state and Nietzsche's. The key difference between Nietzsche and Plato is that for the latter the philosopher-king is one who has access to universal truth, who discovers the truth, whereas for Nietzsche he is fundamentally, in his early writings anyway, an artist who invents the truth. For Nietzsche, it is necessary to recognize that, in the modern age, belief in unconditional authority and absolute truth is on the wane. What is distinctive of the modern age is the secularization of political authority:

> 'In the sphere of higher culture there will always have to be sovereign authority, to be sure – but this sovereign authority will hereafter lie in the hands of the oligarchs of the spirit.'
>
> Human, All Too Human, 261

What is needed to cure social ills 'is not forcible redistribution of property but a gradual transformation of mind: the sense of justice must grow greater in everyone and the instinct for violence weaker' (*HAH*, 452).

The capacity to build a new future depends on an ability to see continuity with the strength of past traditions. An important passage in *Human, All Too Human*, called 'Religion and Government', notes that the importance of religion in the life of a culture is that it consoles the hearts of individuals in times of loss, deprivation and fear – that is, in times when a government is powerless to alleviate the sufferings of people during such tragedies as famine and war. However, the increase in democracy has seen a parallel decline in the importance of religion and a greater emphasis on the ego. This, Nietzsche stresses, is not 'individualism' or 'existentialism'.

It is a mistake to interpret Nietzsche, as some scholars such as Derrida do, as someone unconcerned with society or politics, but rather only centred on the asocial, isolated individual. Nietzsche is deeply committed to the promotion of high culture and sees the role of the individual in an ancient Greek sense as a citizen, as part of a community. His attack on modernity is an attack on liberal democracy with its atomistic individuals lost at sea with no values or meaning. In this sense, Nietzsche is very much a traditionalist.

With the decline in political absolutism sanctioned by divine law, there is the possibility that the state, too, will break apart as reverence for political authority is lost. Nietzsche hopes that the increase in the secular will lead to a new period of toleration, pluralism and wisdom if chaos and anarchy are to be avoided. Nietzsche, it should be stressed, is not anti-democratic so long as it leaves space for the rare, the unique and the noble. Democracy does not necessarily lead to the death of high culture and noble values, provided that culture and politics can give each other space. Nietzsche believes that democracy is the political form of the modern world which is most able to offer the best protection of culture – that is, of art, of religion, of all creativity. In his letters, he says he is 'speaking of democracy as something yet to come' and favours a social order which 'keeps open all the paths to the accumulation of moderate wealth through work', while preventing 'the sudden or unearned acquisition of riches'.

Nietzsche wishes to preserve a private/public distinction, whereas modern liberal society – although its ideology of the privatization of politics allows individuals a great degree of private freedom – undermines notions of culture and citizenship. Nietzsche's criticisms are levelled against the prevailing democracy of his time, remembering that most of Europe was still autocratic, but was not against a democracy 'yet to come'. This raises interesting debates, occurring in our current time, as to what forms of democracy are possible and a growing awareness that there is not a one-fits-all political system, as has been demonstrated when attempts have been made to impose Western forms of democracy on non-Western states, with devastating consequences. Democratic politics, Nietzsche acknowledges, can promote and further culture and, in the recognition that with modernity comes the absence of any possibility of ethical universality, the best hope for the future is that there exists a culture. What kind of culture this would be is uncertain. Would we all agree that Nietzsche's conception of culture, of high culture, is one we would accept?

Nietzsche's nihilism is his contempt for what he regards as negative or destructive values, such as democracy, feminism, socialism and other features of the modern world. Nietzsche sees these modern ideas as lacking in a positive ethos: they are slave values and as such the products of *ressentiment* (see Chapter 4). But it is wrong to accuse Nietzsche of being a nihilist, for a nihilist is only negative and puts nothing forward in its place, whereas Nietzsche is greatly concerned – in fact, you could consider it his primary mission throughout much of his life – with a need to present new values (even if those new values are a return to ancient values), not simply to get rid of the present ones and put nothing in their place.

As stated above, Nietzsche does resemble Plato in some respects regarding his political views. In fact, *Beyond Good and Evil* contains passages that are remarkably similar, with their descriptions of three classes: first, the spiritual leaders; second, those who aspire to be leaders and for whom future rulers may arise; and third, 'the vast majority who exist to serve and be generally useful and must exist only to that end' (Section 61). Like Plato, mention is not specifically made of the 'fourth class', the slaves, but it seems to be a given that slavery would be required 'in one sense or another' (Section 257). Must we then admit that Nietzsche is an advocate of slavery?

We saw how Nietzsche was later critical of his *The Birth of Tragedy,* which he considered a naive and immature work, and so it may well be that we could forgive his remarks on slavery in 'The Greek State' – written at the same time – as the product of a naive young mind. This cannot be defended, however, as his views remained consistent and he sticks to his guns in his much more mature work *Beyond Good and Evil.* However, it may well be argued that we should not be out to defend or attack Nietzsche, for what he was doing was merely pointing out that culture is, historically speaking, built upon a foundation of cruelty and oppression. If we choose to create a society that is egalitarian and compassionate, we can say goodbye to high culture and hello to reality TV and celebrity chefs. The debate then centres around whether or not it is the case that liberal society does in fact lead to a recognition that all things have value and, therefore, nothing has value. Is twentieth-first-century Western democracy any less cultural than an aristocratic society would be?

Spotlight

It is only relatively recently in Nietzschean scholarship that his views on the importance of the *Volk*, or community, have become more greatly appreciated. Having said that, there are some modern scholars who would nonetheless deny he has such concerns at all. Possibly, this ambiguity is a reflection of Nietzsche's own reluctance to present any kind of 'agenda' in his writings.

The immoralist?

Leaving aside whether or not a liberal democratic society is capable of achieving such cultural peaks, it is still questionable whether Nietzsche is simply stating what he perceives as a fact or whether he wants to go further and prescribe an aristocratic society with slavery 'in one sense or another'. The fact that Nietzsche considers himself the bringer of an urgent message to humanity makes him come across as the messenger of 'ought' rather than just 'is'. He writes of:

'... virtuous stupidity; what are needed are unwavering beat-keepers of the slow spirit so that the believers of the great common faith stay together and go on dancing their dance; it is an exigency of the first order which commands and demands.'

The Gay Science, 76

There is definitely an 'ought' here, an 'exigency', a necessity for 'beat-keepers' of 'virtuous stupidity' so that Nietzsche's higher men can 'dance their dance'. Are these 'virtuously stupid' Nietzsche's oppressed slaves who live in misery so that the select few can live in joy? Nietzsche often referred to himself as an 'immoralist' in the sense that he rejected Christian morality, but a number of scholars have gone so far as to say that Nietzsche is, in fact, an immoralist of the highest order – that is, he defends views that are morally abhorrent to most people, such as the support of slavery. If this is indeed the case, it brings into serious question why anybody would wish to praise Nietzsche's moral philosophy.

The modern philosopher Julian Young has argued against this understanding of Nietzsche's immoralism, stating that a better term to describe Nietzsche's moral outlook is paternalism. While paternalism may not be a particularly fashionable view these days, it is in keeping with Nietzsche's time and, indeed, most of human history. This may not help anyone who wants to argue that Nietzsche was ahead of his time, but what this book has hopefully demonstrated is that Nietzsche was not quite the radical existentialist that he has often been made out to be, but more of a traditionalist who looks back, rather than forward, for his values. Nietzsche is paternalistic in that he believes most people are better off being subordinate and led by stronger figures. Incidentally, as will be considered overleaf, 'most people' was particularly relevant to women. While his views on the masses may be misplaced in relation to modern morality, this does not make him immoral, given his concern for the welfare of these masses, even if he refers to them mockingly as 'virtuously stupid'!

Other philosophers, notably John Rawls and Philippa Foot, have argued that Nietzsche is not at all concerned with the well-being of the masses and that his only concern is for his Socratic elite. Section 258 of *Beyond Good and Evil* does seem to defend this view:

> 'When for example an aristocracy like pre-Revolutionary France tosses away its privileges with sublime revulsion and sacrifices itself to its excess of moral feeling, this is corruption: it was really only the final act of that centuries-long corruption that caused the aristocracy to abandon its tyrannical authority bit by bit and reduce itself to a function *of the monarchy (and ultimately in fact to its ornament and showpiece). The crucial thing about a good and healthy aristocracy, however, is that it does* not *feel that it is a function (whether of monarchy or community) but rather an* essence *and highest justification – and that therefore it has no misgivings in condoning the sacrifice of a vast number of people who must* for its sake *be oppressed and diminished into incomplete people, slaves, tools.'*
>
> *Beyond Good and Evil,* 258

In the same section, Nietzsche goes on to compare society to 'scaffolding' for the greatest to climb. How can this be seen as anything other than a justification for using the masses as 'tools' for the elite? The best defence, again offered by Julian Young, is that Nietzsche does not say here that it is 'my belief', but again is simply stating facts of the past in an anthropological way. What Nietzsche is doing in this section is blaming the French aristocrats for being so complacent and arrogant and 'tossing away' their privileges, thus leading to the collapse of society, to decay and 'corruption'. He is not, in fact, endorsing this particular kind of aristocracy. Nietzsche's more 'spiritual aristocracy' would be of a different kind altogether: one in which the elite would be there for the benefit of society as a whole, not to use them for its own ends. This reading can only be understood in the context of other things Nietzsche has said and cannot stand alone, in particular (though by no means exclusively) in *Beyond Good and Evil* (see below).

On women

We have seen that one reading of Nietzsche is that his views
on slavery are somewhat ambiguous, and that it may well be
understood as Nietzsche's own anthropological approach to
how aristocracies have operated in the past. He then uses this as
his model to propose a new state led by a spiritual aristocracy
which, being elitist, would, no doubt, be hierarchical but also for
the benefit of all. This will still leave a bad taste in the mouth of
many modern readers brought up in a liberal, egalitarian society,
but Nietzsche has given his reasons – whether you agree with him
or not – why a liberal, atomized society is actually a lot worse.

Case study: comments on women in *Beyond Good and Evil*

'A deep man, on the other hand, deep both in spirit and in desire,
deep in a benevolence that is capable of rigour and harshness and
easily mistaken for them, can think about women only like an Orient:
he has to conceive of woman as a possession, as securable property,
as something predetermined for service and completed in it.' (238)

'In no other age have men ever treated the weaker sex with such
respect as in our own – it is part of our democratic inclinations and
basic taste, as is our irreverence for old age. Is it any wonder that
this respect is already being abused? They want more; they are
learning to make demands; they end by considering that modicum
of respect almost irritating, preferring to compete, or even to battle
for their rights: let's just say women are becoming shameless.' (239)

'Women want to be autonomous: and to that end they have begun
to enlighten men about "women per se" – that is one of the worst
signs of progress in Europe's overall uglification.' (232)

'Stupidity in the kitchen; women as cooks; the frightful
thoughtlessness that goes into providing nourishment for families
and heads of households! Women don't understand what food
means – and yet they want to be cooks! If women were sentient
beings they would in their thousands of years of cooking experience
have discovered the most important physiological facts and taken
over the healing art!' (234)

Nietzsche's masses will, seemingly, be heavily populated by women, according to his views in *Beyond Good and Evil*. Like his views on slavery, the best we can say perhaps is that this is, again, not Nietzsche being immoral but being paternalistic or, perhaps more accurately, patriarchal.

However, this still seems unsatisfactory and does not get at a key question here: why, if Nietzsche is actually traditionalist, elitist, aristocratic, anti-egalitarian and sexist, does he appeal so much to modern liberal, free-thinking men and women? While part of this appeal may well be due to Nietzsche's unique and modern style, his clever use of metaphor, irony, ambiguity and so on, it is certainly inadequate to be satisfied with this and simply ignore the actual content.

Nietzsche, for his part, was out to criticize European feminism, in the same way that he attacked just about everything in Europe during his time: nothing escaped his scattergun. Feminism was just one of those features of modernity, with its origins in the French Revolution and its ideas of equality. Nietzsche could, and indeed has, been conscripted into the feminist cause to some extent by feminist scholars emphasizing Nietzsche's attack on equality as an enemy of the Noble spirit: the aristocratic figure, or the philosopher-king, if you like. Seen in one context, the Noble spirit can encompass women as well as men, in that it is essentially an attack on nineteenth-century egalitarianism that diminishes self-worth rather than women as such. However, this may be seen as a somewhat generous reading of Nietzsche.

Jacques Derrida, an important philosopher on Nietzsche mentioned in the Introduction, comments in his significant work *Spurs* on the following remark made by Nietzsche in *Beyond Good and Evil*:

> 'Assuming that truth is a woman – what then? Is there not reason to suspect that all philosophers, in so far as they were dogmatists, have known very little about women?'
>
> *Beyond Good and Evil*, Preface

Derrida sees this as arguing that, in the same way as there is no single, unitary Truth as such, there is no single, unitary Woman as such. Nietzsche's criticism of feminism, then, is that it attempts to determine an essence of womanhood, which is doing the same thing as men do to women: that is, women are 'this or that'. In fact, by woman attempting to define herself, she therefore limits her own freedom for ambiguity. Nietzsche's Noble spirit is one that is an artist, in the sense that he (or she?) creates himself (or herself) and is not limited by any universal essence. It is this understanding of Nietzsche that has its roots in **existentialism**, most succinctly defined by Jean-Paul Sartre as 'existence precedes essence' (see Chapter 11). Again, however, this seems like a very generous reading of Nietzsche, given what Nietzsche actually says about women in such a deriding manner. It does not seem likely that Nietzsche was talking metaphorically here or, as Derrida suggests, that Nietzsche is actually writing with a feminine voice.

The philosophers of the future

In *Beyond Good and Evil* especially, Nietzsche talks of the philosophers of the future, and it has been argued in this chapter that there would be political implications involved (although see below for dispute over this). Nietzsche's comments on these leaders – especially given the German word *Führer* – has resulted in many misunderstandings, with visions of blond Aryan beasts oppressing the masses. It still begs the question, nonetheless, who these philosophers of the future would be and what exactly they would do. Those who would argue against any political agenda at all would see these philosophers as essentially freethinkers, artists, musicians and so on, whereas Nietzsche's use of such terms in *Beyond Good and Evil* as 'commanders and lawgivers' (*BGE*, 211) seems more akin to Plato's philosopher-kings legislating over a new form of society:

Nietzsche's philosopher of the future is not just a codifier of values, but a creator of values, a lawgiver, a legislator, and this is why Nietzsche sees figures of history like Napoleon as a philosopher more than he does, say, Kant. Like Plato's philosopher–kings, Nietzsche's philosophers will be compelled into action, although the temptation to retreat into solitude through disgust with society will be great. In many respects, the new philosopher will be like Zarathustra, compelled to go down and encourage people to act. He will be the bad conscience of his age – disagreeing with the majority opinions – and will be derided as such. These new philosophers will also be experimenters, not dogmatic in their views. In a Darwinian sense, many will not succeed in their attempts, but it is hoped that years, if not generations, of experimentation will lead to a new age of stability, rather like the Laws of Manu (see below), which Nietzsche also saw as the stable product of many years of empirical experimentation.

Does Nietzsche have political views?

Spotlight

Ultimately, Nietzsche's primary concern was with culture, and whatever heightened this was quite acceptable as far as he was concerned. Looking at democracy as it existed in Nietzsche's time, this seemed to achieve the opposite, or so he believed.

As it is hoped has been made clear in this chapter, Nietzsche argued for a hierarchical society – certainly not a democratic one – in which at the top of the pyramid would be his philosophers of the future, his oligarchs of the spirit. This he discusses in *Beyond Good and Evil*, but another very interesting passage can be found in his later work *The Anti-Christ*, in which he praises the Laws of Manu. These laws are Hindu in origin and date back some 2,000 years, with codes concerning, among other things, the caste system. Consequently, it is anathema to the modern liberal mind. It is no surprise, therefore, that Nietzsche praises it so! He says the following of the Laws of Manu:

'At a certain point in the evolution of a people the most enlightened, that is to say the most reflective and far-sighted class, declares the experience in accordance with which the people is to live – that it can live – to be fixed and settled. Their objective is to bring home the richest and completest harvest from the ages of experimentation and bad experience. What, consequently, is to be prevented above all is the continuation of experimenting, the perpetuation ad infinitum of the fluid condition of values, tests, choices, criticizing of values.'

The Anti-Christ, 57

Here Nietzsche is piling praise on a hierarchical system not too dissimilar from Plato's concept of the state ruled by philosopher–kings, and it is no surprise that Nietzsche himself makes this comparison, substituting Plato's philosopher–kings, with their mystical vision of the Forms, for his own life-affirming Supermen.

It has been argued that, in the same way that Nietzsche seems to praise Islam as a way to contrast it with sickly Christianity, he is doing the same with the Laws of Manu by stating that even this is better than Christianity, and Nietzsche was actually quite critical of Manu in his unpublished notes. But, again, we need to ask why he chose not to publish his criticisms and must be wary of remarks he makes in notes not intended for public consumption. Rather, Nietzsche sees the Laws of Manu as something of a paradigm: as a model, an empirical attempt, to achieve an ideal, while also privately at least acknowledging its flaws. Nietzsche advocates a hierarchical society, but also one much better, more natural than the one Manu or Plato offer.

Key ideas

Existentialism: the philosophical movement that emphasizes human freedom

Laws of Manu: a treatise on law and government composed probably over a period of time (around 200 BCE to 200 CE) in India

Volk: German word for 'the people' or 'the community'

Things to remember

▶ Nietzsche certainly had political views despite the claim by some scholars that he was not concerned with such matters.

▶ *The Birth of Tragedy* was originally intended to involve a discussion of politics. What was to be part of the book became a separate essay called 'The Greek State'. 'The Greek State' is a work of cultural criticism, particularly aimed at the contemporary phenomenon of modernity.

▶ Nietzsche was, on the whole, critical of democracy as it was beginning to emerge in the Europe of his time. However, Nietzsche spoke of a new form of democracy, and so it would be wrong to say that he was against democracy entirely, rather certain forms of democracy.

▶ His main criticism of democracy was that it can be 'levelling', and so does not allow for great men and great culture to flourish.

▶ Nietzsche's views on democracy are not that dissimilar from those of Plato.

▶ Rather than regard Nietzsche as immoral, perhaps he is better described as 'paternalistic' in his views on such things as slavery and women.

▶ Nietzsche's philosophers of the future would not only be artists, musicians and writers, but would also be creators of values and legislators. Political leaders, therefore, are a possibility.

Fact-check

1 Which ancient society invented democracy?
- **a** The Egyptians
- **b** The Greeks
- **c** The Aztecs
- **d** The Romans

2 What is the name of Nietzsche's short essay outlining his political views?
- **a** 'The Democratic State'
- **b** 'The Elite State'
- **c** 'The German State'
- **d** 'The Greek State'

3 Whose philosophy do Nietzsche's political views most resemble?
- **a** Aristotle's
- **b** Plato's
- **c** Hobbes's
- **d** Mill's

4 What does the term *Volk* mean?
- **a** Community
- **b** A German car
- **c** The Greek city-state
- **d** King

5 Which philosopher regards Nietzsche's moral views as 'paternalistic'?
- **a** John Rawls
- **b** Philippa Foot
- **c** Julian Young
- **d** Jacques Derrida

6 In which of Nietzsche's works will you find the following opening: 'Assuming that truth is a woman – what then?'
- **a** *Beyond Good and Evil*
- **b** *The Birth of Tragedy*
- **c** *Ecce Homo*
- **d** *The Anti-Christ*

7 What is the name of the philosopher who defined existentialism as 'existence precedes essence'?

   a Albert Camus

   b Søren Kierkegaard

   c Martin Buber

   d Jean-Paul Sartre

8 What are the Laws of Manu?

   a Laws created by Nietzsche's Zarathustra

   b Laws of the Prussian state at the time of Nietzsche

   c Laws of Hindu origin

   d Laws of Persian origin

Dig deeper

Keith Ansell-Pearson, *An Introduction to Nietzsche as Political Thinker: The Perfect Nihilist* (Cambridge: CUP, 1994)

Keith Ansell-Pearson, *Nietzsche and Political Thought*, Bloomsbury Studies in Continental Philosophy (London: Bloomsbury Academic, 2013)

Kelly A. Oliver and Marilyn Pearsall (eds), *Feminist Interpretations of Friedrich Nietzsche (Rereading the Canon)* (University Park, PA: Pennsylvania State University Press, 1998)

Paul Patton, *Nietzsche, Feminism and Political Theory* (London: Routledge, 1993)

Julian Young, *Nietzsche's Philosophy of Religion* (Cambridge: CUP, 2006)

11

Nietzsche's legacy

In this chapter you will learn:

▶ *the reasons why Nietzsche became associated with Nazism*

▶ *about the influence Nietzsche had on French twentieth-century philosophy*

▶ *about his influence on the analytic tradition*

▶ *about other influences, especially on art and literature.*

It has been said that Nietzsche was in no way a racist, except perhaps towards his own nation, the Germans. More accurately, he hated what Germany had become: a nation of nationalists rather than 'good Europeans' who, worse still, were discriminatory towards others. It is a sad irony, therefore, that he became the official German philosopher of the Nazi period.

Needless to say, after the Second World War, serious academic study of Nietzsche was neglected because few wished to be associated with the 'Nazi philosopher'. However, since the second half of the twentieth century Nietzsche's influence has grown, and his ideas have had a major impact on many artists and writers in France and elsewhere, and also on the analytic tradition of Britain and the United States.

Nazism

'Listen to me for I am thus and thus. Do not, above all, confound me with what I am not!'

Ecce Homo, Foreword

During the First World War, Elisabeth Nietzsche proclaimed her brother as an imperialist and a warrior who would have been proud of the Germans' cause. She arranged for copies of *Thus Spoke Zarathustra* to be sent to the troops.

However, it was with the arrival of the dictators that she was really able to promote Nietzsche's philosophy. She heard that the Italian fascist dictator Mussolini had claimed that Nietzsche had been a great influence on his politics, and so she made a point of establishing a regular correspondence with him. Mussolini took the notion of the Superman to mean anyone who stands out from the crowd and controls his own destiny. In fact, he saw himself as one of these Supermen, and Elisabeth praised him as the new Caesar.

When Elisabeth chose to stage a play written by Mussolini at the Nietzsche Archive, the Italian leader was unable to attend. However, the leader of the National Socialist Party, Adolf Hitler, was present that night. This was her first introduction and she immediately fell under his spell. It was in 1933 at the Bayreuth Festival on the fiftieth anniversary of Wagner's death that Elisabeth Nietzsche and Adolf Hitler discussed Nietzsche's philosophy. Nietzsche later became the official philosopher of Germany, giving Nazism the intellectual credibility it otherwise lacked. In fact, Nietzsche's own comments on Germans and the German nation might well have resulted in imprisonment or worse during the period of Nazi Germany if they had ever been allowed to be aired in public.

Aside from his sister's active encouragement, there were other reasons for associating Nietzsche with Hitler:

▶ **Nietzsche's association with the Wagner family**
Richard Wagner himself was an anti-Semite and the Wagners as a whole have been associated with National Socialism. As a consequence, any disciple of Wagner is an implied disciple of National Socialism, despite Nietzsche distancing himself from Wagner's influence in the late 1870s. For example, one of the leading figures and theoretical inspirations for Nazi thought was actually an Englishman, Houston Stewart Chamberlain (1855–1927), who became a zealous Germanophile and, significantly, wed Richard Wagner's youngest daughter, Eva. Chamberlain wrote an extensive anti-Semitic text called *Foundations of the Nineteenth Century* (1899), which was a bestseller during the rise of Hitler alongside *Thus Spoke Zarathustra*, so these two books were linked in the German mind.

▶ **The similarity of Nietzsche's writing style to Hitler's**
The similarity of Nietzsche's caustic writing style to Hitler's was especially strong during the last two years of Nietzsche's sane life, when he became much more rhetorical, combative and violent in tone (see case study below). The language of hatred and venom used by Nietzsche in his attack on Christians is not dissimilar from the language used by Hitler to attack the Jews. In *Mein Kampf* (*My Struggle*), for example, Hitler used terms such as 'parasite' and 'spiritual pestilence'. However, whereas Nietzsche's solution to the problem of prevalent Jewish and Christian values was largely peaceful in tone, focusing on a revaluation of values, Hitler's

solution was, alas, far more extreme. While their concerns were essentially the same in that both strived for a healthy culture and looked to certain sections of humanity that were considered unhealthy, they differed drastically in their methods and focus.

Case study: Nietzsche's violent language

'The priest himself is recognized for what he is: the most dangerous kind of parasite, the actual poison-spider of life.' (*The Anti-Christ*, 38)

'[St Paul was] … a hate-obsessed false-coiner [counterfeiter].' (*The Anti-Christ*, 42)

'Wherever there is anything small and sick and scabby, there they crawl like lice; and only my disgust stops me from cracking them.' (*Thus Spoke Zarathrustra*, 'Of the Virtue That Makes Small', Part 3.3)

'One does well to put on gloves on reading the New Testament.' (*The Anti-Christ*, 46)

'The ascetic ideal, with its sublime moral cult, with its brilliant and irresponsible use of the emotions for holy purposes, has etched itself on the memory of mankind terribly and unforgettably. I can think of no development that has had a more pernicious effect upon the health of the race, and especially the European race, than this.'
On the Genealogy of Morals, Essay 3, 21

▶ **Nietzsche's belief in community, in the *Volk***
Another possible reason for Nietzsche's association with National Socialism is that, although he was anti-German in many of his remarks, he was a strong believer in community, in the *Volk*. Nietzsche contrasts this form of German Romanticism with the seeming emptiness and plurality of modernism. The poet Friedrich Hölderlin (1770–1843) – whom Nietzsche read voraciously – wrote of the 'destitution'

of modernity and Nietzsche shared this hostility towards modernity, with its emphasis on Enlightenment reason, and stressed instead the importance of community and the role of religion within it (see Chapter 9), but he distanced himself from the Romantic association with nationalism. *Volk*ish thinking became indelibly linked with German nationalism and figures such as Heinrich Riehl (1823–97), Paul de Lagarde (1827–91) and, importantly, Richard Wagner. Coupled with this German nationalism was anti-Semitism. Despite Nietzsche's own remarks, he was inevitably associated with these figures.

Twentieth-century French philosophy

> *'It is really only small number of older Frenchmen to whom I return again and again: I believe only in French culture and consider everything else in Europe that calls itself "culture" a misunderstanding, not to speak of German culture...'*
> Ecce Homo, 'Why I Am So Clever', 3

It could reasonably be argued that to understand twentieth-century French philosophy you have to understand Nietzsche. As already stated, Nietzsche hated German nationalism and, to some extent, was not that keen on Germany either. Nietzsche, travelling from one country to another for much of his life, was a true European, and it was French culture especially that he had a soft spot for, despite the fact he spent little time there. Of course, he likewise often spoke admiringly of Islamic countries and culture, yet never spent any time at all in an Islamic country.

For its part, France was slow to take on Nietzsche in the philosophy departments, but when it did, it did so by storm. In fact, it was not so much the philosophy departments that took up Nietzsche to begin with, but the country's writers and artists. One such writer, although something of a philosopher, was Georges Bataille (1897–1962). Under the influence of Nietzsche's views on the Apollonian–Dionysian dichotomy (see Chapter 3), Bataille presented a vision of the world as one that should be Dionysian in character: one in which there is overflowing ecstasy, excess and waste. He believed that the production of waste products was a necessity of life, and so he would have despaired at modern-day attempts to recycle and create a self-contained equilibrium as the equivalent of an Apollonian, rational monster.

JEAN-PAUL SARTRE (1905–80)

This view of the world as essentially a result of waste products, of a world of dead bodies, flies, dirt, mucus, urine, pus, phlegm, vomit, dandruff and so on was the reality portrayed by the existentialist philosopher and writer Jean-Paul Sartre. This world is difficult to face unless we comfort ourselves by creating ideals – illusions in which to cope with the mundane and horrific. The experience of 'nausea' described in his novel *Nausea* is actually a form of enlightenment, an awareness of what it means to be alive. In *Nausea*, the character of Roquentin encounters the world of people and inanimate objects and sees things as having the stamp of his existence upon them. This gives existence a nauseating quality, and 'nausea' is an expression also used by Nietzsche in works such as *Thus Spoke Zarathustra* and *Beyond Good and Evil*. Coupled with this concept of nausea is the realization that attempts to deal with objects, situations and people in a rational matter are absurd, and this led to a whole school of Absurdist literature.

ALBERT CAMUS (1913–60)

In the case of the Algerian-born French author, philosopher and journalist Albert Camus, for life to be meaningful we must live every moment like a person who has just come out of prison and smells the fresh air, feels the sunlight and the ground below. This life-affirming attitude is akin to Nietzsche's, and Camus considered his thoughts to be a reaction against nihilism. While Camus tried to disassociate himself from any philosophical schools, he was, as a result of his own writings, inevitably linked with existentialism and the Absurd. While Camus never provides a specific doctrine of the Absurd, he nonetheless writes of experiencing the Absurd in, for example, his novel *The Outsider* and his essay 'The Myth of Sisyphus'. In this essay, Camus highlights the absurdity of existence by demonstrating that we live a life of paradox: on the one hand valuing our own lives and striving to make something of them, while on the other hand being aware that we are all mortal and so our endeavours will ultimately come to nothing.

Camus's aim was not to depress everybody, but rather to consider how we face such absurdity. In fact, he didn't think that life was meaningless: meaning can be created by our own decisions and perspectives, even if this is a temporary thing. This focus on no universals and the death of God – and therefore the death of any kind of absolutes – again was the concern of Nietzsche, who likewise rejected nihilism as an option. Camus's philosophical novel *The Fall* considers the will to power in the context of the weak who, as a final resort, gain a sense of being better than others because they admit they are riddled with guilt.

HENRI BERGSON (1859–1941)

The Two Sources of Morality and Religion (1932) is the French philosopher Bergson's only published work that mentions Nietzsche by name, but Bergson's philosophy is Nietzschean in many respects. Like Nietzsche, Bergson sets out to reverse Platonism by presenting what has been referred to as process philosophy. That is to say, philosophy does not unravel permanent truths – which would be Platonism – but rather truth is a process involving time, perception, change, memory and intuition. Like Nietzsche's critique of modernity, Bergson attacked the mechanistic philosophy of his time, arguing for intelligence as evolutionary and adaptable. Interestingly, Bergson's philosophy had a major influence on the Greek novelist Nikos Kazantzakis (1885–1957), who also read Nietzsche and produced a version of process theology, expressed in his major work *Zorba the Greek*. According to Kazantzakis, when we look at the source of religion we see that God is the product of whatever people value.

GILLES DELEUZE (1925–95)

Nietzsche's influence on the French philosopher Deleuze is particularly (though by no means exclusively) evident in his ethics and politics, in that he took up Nietzsche's emphasis on ethical naturalism (see Chapter 4). Like Nietzsche, Deleuze sets out to understand the moral actions and beliefs of people as deriving from their desires and quest for power. To live well is to fully express one's power – that is, to go to the limits of your own potential rather than look for transcendent, universal standards to live by. In *Essays Critical and Clinical*, Deleuze outlines what we must do in the face of a world that is one of flux and difference: 'Herein, perhaps, lies the secret: to bring into existence and not to judge. If it is so disgusting to judge, it is not because everything is of equal value, but on the contrary because what has value can be made or distinguished only by defying judgement. What expert judgement, in art, could ever bear on the work to come?'

MICHEL FOUCAULT (1926–84)

Perhaps no other French philosopher is more closely associated with Nietzsche than Foucault. Like Nietzsche, he interpreted the world in terms of the will to power and, again, like Nietzsche, had a genealogical agenda that he referred to as 'archaeology': an experimental method that he employed to study aspects of modernity. In the same way as an archaeologist literally digs to put together how a society lived, Foucault 'digs' at the form and content of language used in fields of knowledge to reveal the hidden interests of those engaged in discourse – that is, in the dissemination of knowledge. For example, as he states in his work *Discipline and Punish*, when experts (lawyers, psychologists, parole officers and so on) judge on a person's criminality, Foucault sees this as an exercise of power over the criminal. In actual fact, Foucault argues, there is no objective valuation of what a criminal is, and what counts as criminal behaviour in one culture and at one time can be regarded as legal in another.

Like Nietzsche, Foucault attacked Enlightenment attitudes to such concepts as inalienable rights, for Foucault would argue that there is no such thing as a universal good. While arguing for no absolutes, Foucault would not allow himself to be drawn into an ethical system or a political agenda. Foucault saw it as his mission to investigate, not to advocate.

The analytic tradition

The **analytic** movement dominated philosophy in Britain and
the United States for most of the second half of the twentieth
century. Like existentialism, it is difficult to identify specific
tenets of this movement, although most analytic philosophers
argue that the primary aim of philosophy is, or should be, to
look to how language is used. Language, it is argued, is the
basis for all our knowledge, and so when we use concepts, the
important thing is to consider how those concepts are used in
the context of language.

It is interesting that, whereas existentialism tends to emphasize
the irrational and emotional side, the analytic tradition is
much more rationalist and logical. Yet Nietzsche succeeds in
straddling both traditions. Although Nietzsche is not such
a direct influence upon the analytic tradition, much of his
philosophy is considered to be firmly within this tradition,
particularly his criticism of past philosophers for preoccupying
themselves with metaphysical questions and also his view that it
is not whether something is 'true' or 'false' that is important but
whether a claim makes sense. Further, Nietzsche understood the
importance of language in defining our world.

One branch of the analytic movement is called **logical positivism**,
which adopted a criterion of meaning which stated that, unless
a statement can be verified by experience (for example, 'all
bachelors are happy') or is true by definition (for example, 'a
bachelor is an unmarried man'), then it is meaningless. This
inevitably results in metaphysical statements being discarded as
irrelevant to philosophy because such statements as 'God is wise'

cannot be proven by experience and nor is it by definition the case that 'God' and 'wisdom' are synonymous (although some have argued that in fact they are synonymous).

Case study: Thomas Altizer (1927–)

The influence of Nietzsche on theology is also evident in the writings of Thomas Altizer, who helped to create a 'death of God' theology. This may strike some as something of an oxymoron, but it was nonetheless an attempt to address Nietzsche's concern that the Christianity of the time was leading to nihilism. By God's 'death', Altizer is actually referring to the crucifixion of Jesus Christ, which, he says, resulted in the pouring out of God's spirit into the world. God's spirit, then, is not transcendent any more, but immanent: it exists in the material world, in the here and now.

Art and literature

Spotlight

You will find, if you haven't already, that Nietzsche's name will regularly crop up in literature, film and other media. He is eminently quotable, but, alas, he is still often misunderstood and it pays to have a better understanding of what he really meant.

Other than those already mentioned, such as Kazantzakis, Sartre and Camus, writers influenced by Nietzsche and who have also written about him include Thomas Mann (1875–1955), Hermann Hesse (1877–1962) and George Bernard Shaw (1856–1950).

▶ Thomas Mann was particularly interested in Nietzsche's views on the connection between sickness and creativity, which comes across especially in his novel *The Magic Mountain*. Like Nietzsche, Mann argued that disease should not be seen in a wholly negative way, because life and great creativity can come out of illness.

▶ Hesse's novel *Steppenwolf* portrays the Nietzschean loner, the 'beast' or 'genius' in the character of Harry Haller who feels out of place in the world of 'everybody'. Hesse lived in Basel for a time, partly because he saw it as the town of Nietzsche.

▶ Shaw's play *Man and Superman* comes directly from Nietzsche's ideas on the Superman.

Other famous writers influenced by Nietzsche include André Malraux (1901–76), André Gide (1869–1951) and Knut Hamsun (1859–1952), while Nietzschean themes crop up among the beat poets such as Allen Ginsberg (1926–97) and Gary Snyder (1930–).

The Jewish American painter Mark Rothko (1903–70) was especially influenced by *The Birth of Tragedy*. Rothko believed that the mission of art was to address the need for modern man to be redeemed from the horrors of life through myth. Rothko regarded himself as a mythmaker, as is evident from the titles of so many of his paintings: *Antigone*, *Oedipus*, *The Sacrifice of Iphigenia*, *The Furies*, *Altar of Orpheus* and so on.

Many other thinkers, philosophers and psychologists have been influenced by the ideas and the philosophy of Nietzsche:

▶ In Russia, the **Symbolists** – who proclaimed art to be the new religion and the Superman to be the artist – adopted Nietzsche's philosophy.

▶ Nietzsche's future-oriented philosophy, of man as a bridge to a higher man, influenced revolutionary thinkers such as Trotsky.

▶ The psychologist Sigmund Freud (1856–1939) thought highly of Nietzsche, as did Carl Jung (1875–1961).

▶ The Austrian psychologist Alfred Adler (1870–1937) founded a school of 'individual psychology' where the emphasis on power dynamics is rooted in the philosophy of Nietzsche.

▶ American novelist, philosopher and playwright Ayn Rand (1905–82) was likewise inspired by the writings of Nietzsche.

Nietzsche, no doubt, will continue to influence new generations on a variety of different levels, whether due to his artistic style, the fact that a reader can pick on one profound sentence and write a novel around it, or due to his philosophy specifically, which has outlived the man and his age and is as applicable to today's society as it was to Nietzsche's time and the horrors that engulfed Europe in the twentieth century.

Key ideas

Absurdism: a term common in existential philosophy and referring to the seeming conflict between our search for meaning in the world with our actual experience as lacking in any value

Analytic: the tradition in philosophy that emphasizes the importance of language in our understanding of the world

Logical positivism: an expression of the analytic tradition in philosophy that argues that statements are meaningless if they cannot be verified

Symbolism: a late nineteenth-century movement in art with its origins in France, Russia and Belgium

Things to remember

▶ Nietzsche always considered himself a 'good European' rather than a German.

▶ His sister Elisabeth promoted Nietzsche as the philosopher of National Socialism. Because of his 'links' with Nazism, Nietzsche was largely neglected after the Second World War.

▶ Serious study of Nietzsche did not occur until the 1960s.

▶ In particular, Nietzsche is often presented as a precursor of French existentialism.

▶ The writings of the French philosopher Michel Foucault are also influenced by Nietzsche.

▶ The importance of language, which Nietzsche stressed, became a dominant theme in philosophy in Britain and America in what is known as analytic philosophy.

▶ Nietzsche has had an impact on such diverse writers as Thomas Mann, Hermann Hesse and George Bernard Shaw.

▶ To this day, Nietzsche's influence can be seen in literature, media and other arts, as well as in twenty-first-century philosophy.

Fact-check

1 Which one of the following is *not* a reason why Nietzsche is associated with Hitler?
- **a** Elisabeth Nietzsche's encouragement
- **b** Nietzsche's association with the Wagners
- **c** Friedrich Nietzsche's own support for National Socialism
- **d** Nietzsche's views on the *Volk*

2 Which French writer was influenced by Nietzsche's Dionysian philosophy?
- **a** Jean Genet
- **b** Georges Bataille
- **c** Françoise Sagan
- **d** Marcel Proust

3 Which one of the following novels did Jean-Paul Sartre write?
- **a** *Nausea*
- **b** *Sickness unto Death*
- **c** *Despair*
- **d** *Sick and Tired*

4 Which one of the following novels did Albert Camus write?
- **a** *Nausea*
- **b** *The Outsider*
- **c** *The Absurd*
- **d** *The Invisible Man*

5 What is the name of Albert Camus's famous philosophical essay on absurdity?
- **a** 'The Myth of the Absurd'
- **b** 'The Myth of Dionysus'
- **c** 'The Myth of Camus'
- **d** 'The Myth of Sisyphus'

6 What is the name of Henri Bergson's work that mentions Nietzsche?
- **a** *The Two Sources of Morality and Religion*
- **b** *The Two Gods of Apollo and Dionysus*
- **c** *The Two Sources of Faith and Knowledge*
- **d** *The Two Realities of Birth and Death*

7 Who wrote *Zorba the Greek*?

   a Andreas Karkavitsas

   b Panos Koutrouboussis

   c Nikos Kazantzakis

   d Menis Koumandareas

8 What is the theology that Thomas Altizer is particularly renowned for?

   a The Death of Morals Theology

   b The Death of God Theology

   c The Death of Nietzsche Theology

   d The Death of the Church Theology

9 Which one of the following writers was *not* influenced by Nietzsche?

   a Thomas Mann

   b Hermann Hesse

   c Charles Dickens

   d George Bernard Shaw

10 Which one of the following painters was influenced by Nietzsche's philosophy?

   a Leonardo da Vinci

   b Caravaggio

   c Raphael

   d Mark Rothko

Dig deeper

Albert Camus, *The Myth of Sisyphus* (London: Penguin, 2005)

Hermann Hesse, *Steppenwolf* (London: Penguin Modern Classics, 2001)

Aaron Ridley, *Routledge Philosophy Guidebook to Nietzsche on Art* (London: Routledge, 2007)

Jean-Paul Sartre, *Nausea* (London: Penguin, 2000)

Nietzsche's writings: abbreviations and translations used

AC: Twilight of the Idols and the Anti-Christ, trans. by R.J. Hollingdale (London: Penguin, 1990)

BGE: Beyond Good and Evil, trans. by Marion Faber (Oxford: Oxford World Classics, 2008)

BT: The Birth of Tragedy, trans. by Shaun Whiteside (London: Penguin, 1993)

EH: Ecce Homo, trans. by R.J. Hollingdale (London: Penguin, 1992)

GM: On the Genealogy of Morals, trans. by Douglas Smith (Oxford: Oxford World's Classics, 2008)

GS: The Gay Science, trans. by Walter Kaufmann (London: Random House, 1991)

GSt: 'The Greek State', in vol. 2 of *The Complete Works of Friedrich Nietzsche*, ed. O. Levy, trans. by M.A. Mügge (London: T.A. Foulis, 1911)

HAH: Human, All Too Human, trans. by Marion Faber (London: Penguin, 1994)

TI: Twilight of the Idols and the Anti-Christ, trans. by R.J. Hollingdale (London: Penguin, 1990)

TSZ: Thus Spoke Zarathustra, trans. by R.J. Hollingdale (London: Penguin, 1974)

UM: Untimely Meditations, trans. by R.J. Hollingdale (Cambridge: CUP, 1997)

WP: The Will to Power, trans. by Walter Kaufmann and R.J. Hollingdale (London: Random House, 1973)

Timeline of important events in Nietzsche's life

1844 Friedrich Wilhelm Nietzsche born on 15 October in Röcken, a small village near Lützen.

1849 Death of Nietzsche's father on 30 July, diagnosed as softening of the brain.

1850 Nietzsche's brother, Ludwig Joseph, dies on 9 January. The family relocates to Naumburg in early April.

1856 Nietzsche writes his first philosophical essay, 'On the Origin of Evil'.

1858 In October he is accepted into the Pforta school.

1862 Together with a few friends, he founds the literary club 'Germania'.

1864 In October he begins studying theological and classical philology in Bonn.

1865 Leaves Bonn and moves to Leipzig to study philology. He has given up on theology. In October he discovers Schopenhauer.

1868 Becomes friends with Wagner.

1869 Appointed to the University of Basel.

1870 Military service as a medic. He falls ill with dysentery and diphtheria.

1872 *The Birth of Tragedy* is published. It is rejected by scholars.

1876 Becomes friends with Rée and attends the first Bayreuth Festival. He makes his mind up to break with Wagner.

1879 Resigns from university teaching and starts his nomadic life.

1881 His first visit to Sils-Maria. Has his great 'inspiration' and writes of eternal recurrence.

1882 Proposes marriage to Lou Salomé twice.

1883 Death of Wagner on 13 February.

1885 Nietzsche's sister marries Bernhard Förster in May.

1889 Nietzsche breaks down and never recovers from mental illness.

1900 Dies on 25 August.

Index

Note: 'FN' is an abbreviation of Friedrich Nietzsche.

Answers

CHAPTER 1	CHAPTER 2	CHAPTER 3	CHAPTER 4
1 c	1 d	1 c	1 b
2 a	2 c	2 a	2 a
3 d	3 b	3 b	3 c
4 a	4 c	4 c	4 b
5 a	5 a	5 a	5 a
6 d	6 b	6 c	6 c
7 a	7 d	7 a	7 d
8 c	8 c	8 b	8 b
9 a	9 b	9 b	9 a
10 b	10 a	10 d	10 c

CHAPTER 5	CHAPTER 7	CHAPTER 9	CHAPTER 11
1 c	1 b	1 c	1 c
2 b	2 c	2 d	2 b
3 a	3 a	3 a	3 a
4 a	4 b	4 a	4 b
5 b	5 c	5 c	5 d
6 d	6 d	6 a	6 a
7 d	7 a	7 c	7 c
8 a	8 a	8 b	8 b
9 b	9 c		9 c
10 b	10 d		10 d

CHAPTER 6	CHAPTER 8	CHAPTER 10
1 c	1 a	1 b
2 b	2 b	2 d
3 c	3 a	3 b
4 a	4 c	4 a
5 b	5 d	5 c
6 b	6 b	6 a
7 c	7 c	7 d
8 d	8 b	8 c
9 a		
10 d		